*Radical Spirit*

# Radical Spirit

### 12 WAYS *to* LIVE *a* FREE *and* AUTHENTIC LIFE

## Joan Chittister

CONVERGENT

NEW YORK

Copyright © 2017 by Joan D. Chittister

All rights reserved.
Published in the United States by Convergent Books,
an imprint of the Crown Publishing Group,
a division of Penguin Random House LLC, New York.
crownpublishing.com

CONVERGENT BOOKS is a registered trademark and its C colophon is a
trademark of Penguin Random House LLC.

Library of Congress Cataloging-in-Publication Data has been applied for.

ISBN 978-0-451-49517-4
Ebook ISBN 978-0-451-49518-1

Printed in the United States of America

*Book design by Anna Thompson*
*Jacket design by Jessie Sayward Bright*
*Jacket lettering by Andy Luce*

10  9  8  7  6  5  4  3  2

First Edition

*This book is dedicated to two Benedictine Sisters whose own spirits give life to the* Radical Spirit *of Benedictine monasticism:*

*Sister Maureen Tobin, my lifelong friend and personal assistant, who embodied and modeled the Benedictine tradition and spirituality this book explores.*

*Sister Mary Lou Kownacki, OSB, has spent her life making this spirituality new again for our own times.*

# Contents

*Radical Spirit*

*Introduction*

# RADICAL SPIRIT

Consider this moment another step in your search for a direction in life that is tried and true. It intends to open your heart and mind to the wellspring of your spiritual self. It can launch you down the path to the fullest kind of human development.

This book is an invitation to internal freedom, to the achievement of the free and authentic life. Most of all, it is rooted in ancient spiritual wisdom that echoes the insights of the ages and, at the same time, sings of a fresher, truer tomorrow.

You are not alone in your quest. The quest for internal freedom and an authentic way of life is common to everyone, to every generation, to every era. But few, other than the ancient mystics, contemplatives, and spiritual seekers of the ages, have had real answers for how to achieve it. Abba Zosimas, a monk in fifth-century Palestine, instructed his disciples very clearly about the inner chains that hold us captive. He told them, "It was well said once by a wise person, that the soul has as many masters as it has passions." And again, the Apostle Peter says, "People are slaves to whatever masters them."

This book is about recognizing what has mastered us and then discovering what it will take to break those chains.

Chained to the present moment by agitation, anger, our addictions, anxieties, fear, stress—whatever the spiritual wrestling match of the day—the pursuit of freedom in a world in perpetual motion is an ongoing one.

In this society, in fact, the search for personal freedom has become big business. Whole industries have been constructed around it—financial consultantships, pharmaceuticals, psychology, tourism—all of them purporting to provide the process for finding personal peace, the tools for removing angst, the way to escape ourselves. But those things never really work. They serve for a while to dampen the groaning, empty pain of it, perhaps. But, in the end, the strictures arise to chafe again. And the first question is always, Why?

Why this impression of internal captivity? Why this sense of emptiness in me? Why my resistance to change? Why the everlasting weight of ghostlike burdens we simply cannot seem to shrug off? And then the second question, Is there no way to deal with this? With what plagues us? Is there no way to escape this? Is there no help, no direction anywhere that can soothe the irritation, subdue the endless ambition, relieve the demands for more in me?

Yes, actually, there is. Self-understanding, a commitment to spiritual growth, a spiritual tradition that has stood the test of time, and a spiritual guide to companion us on the way are the components of the spiritual journey. Each of them requires conscious attention. Each of them is clear.

The understanding of what blocks my growth in life requires deep honesty from me. The struggle to unbind myself from the passions that hold sway over me takes both discipline and support. The search for a spiritual tradition that points me beyond mere religious ritual to a spiritual "true north" gives me an established path to follow. And, finally, the steady presence of a spiritual guide to help me find my way from one question, one step, to the next along the way is a lifelong guarantee of spiritual freedom from the demons within.

And that is why I wrote this book. There is a spiritual document written in the age of Zosimas that gives us a veritable program of liberation. It is a spirituality for the whole of life. Designed to free us from our troubled selves and so from the effects of a self in turmoil, it leads us from one spiritual dimension of life to the next until, eventually, all of life becomes one sacred act.

The Benedictine spirituality that is the foundation of this book is centuries old, but the humility that undergirds monastic spirituality which emerges in Chapter 7 of the sixth-century Rule of Benedict is timeless and lives on to this day. The Twelve Steps of Humility are the centerpiece of this book, in fact. Not because they are old but because they model a way to the freedom of heart and soul which we seek. Best of all, they are sure proof that such freedom is possible in a world where demagoguery is the new political brand, where narcissism is too often misunderstood to be leadership, where pathological individualism in the name of freedom and independence is confused with healthy personal development and spiritual maturity.

This entire document is about growing into the consciousness of God. But, the key to this quest lies, Benedict says, in "humility." These twelve steps are explicit and basic to any group, any relationship, any search for God in life. They're about recognizing the place of God in our personal lives. They're about learning from the wisdom figures we discover in life so that the good they did for us we can go on doing for others. They're about coming to grips with the nagging hungers of the self. They're about realizing the spiritual impact of our own growth on the human relationships around us. They're about becoming authentic human beings, honest about ourselves and free from the narcissistic nonsense that drives the modern age to glory in itself. They're about being free to become the best—the rest—of ourselves without the chains of false expectations.

Grappling with these deep-down, heart-hardening things takes the soulful persistence of a lifetime, and yet, ironically, it is these things which we confront in ourselves that are exactly the parts of ourselves most worthy of our own patience and mercy. The demons with which we struggle as we go through life are the very things that make for our greatness. In fact, it's these that make us holy and tender with others while they bring out the best in us. And it is these for which we need the most guidance, the most understanding, the most support.

The Twelve Steps of Humility, I have learned over the

years, are a spirituality program for a lifetime, the kind that never loses meaning, and so never really gets old. They turn us toward the God of Liberation through all the stages of our growing.

These steps of humility, over fifteen hundred years old now, are guides, tested and found true from one century to another. Like wisdom figures in our midst, centuries later, they have shown me the way to new life over and over again. As my own life shaped and reshaped itself from one phase to another, the degrees of humility forever saved me from myself. They oriented me toward happiness rather than excitement, beyond pleasure to serenity, over and above secular notions of success. But I didn't always know it.

The problem is that at first glance, at first hearing, the modern mind recoils from the very concept on which this process of the liberation of the self from the self is based. Even the word *humility* has an odious tone in a world where the attention on "I" is so much more central than the value of "we."

The sadness is that because, as countercultural as the idea of humility is, everything in our culture militates against our even taking time to explore it. We are afraid to immerse ourselves in a spirituality that strikes at the core of errant ambitions and the dangers of the image building to which our culture calls us. And yet, this very spirituality is meant to free us for the freedom of the spirit we need and for which every person struggles along the way. More than that, humility is our only answer to globalism, to world peace, to economic justice, and to equality. Until humility becomes a factor of life again, the mark of culture and the antidote to narcissism, we condemn ourselves to both personal and national disintegration.

And yet, humility is not, by and large, a Western thing. In too many cases, the spiritual literature on humility has been confused with a penchant for humiliations—and so ignored by modern readers who need the balm and balance of humility most. But not here. Here, in the ancient Rule of Benedict, humility becomes the way to the freedom of heart and simplicity of soul that put the human soul at peace in a confusing, competitive, self-centered, and violent world.

In the Rule of Benedict, a small document of seventy-three short chapters on how to live a holy and loving life, humility is about understanding and realizing the truth of the self. It is how we see ourselves that determines how we see and interact with others. It is how we respond to others that determines how we fare and what we become in the human community. And it is humility that stands to set us free. Free from the ambition that drives us, from the angers that rule us, from the greed that consumes us, from the chains we have mistaken for success and superiority.

Humility in the Rule of Benedict is the spiritual hinge on which the rest of life depends. The full truth of what it means to be spiritual, to be "of God," to be a force in the world for equality, justice, compassion, and human dignity depends on what we mean by humility. In a world torn by violence and a social system built on always grasping for more, humility emerges as the glue that can finally unbind us from ourselves. Then, we are prepared enough to swathe society, family, personal relationships, community, and the human race with care, with justice, with the kind of love that makes life worthwhile for us all.

The Benedictine Rule—like all wisdom literature—is clearly meant for every age. Without the breadth of spiritual perspective this document brings, we are all left to stumble through life with no clear path, no clear goal. We limp along, always seeking God but forever wondering why we must struggle against the lust for perfection, why all the prayers we say are not enough to release us from the albatross of ourselves.

This book is about what it means to develop a deep and definitive spiritual life from day to day. It is ancient Benedictine spirituality that has been a filter through every age and is seen here through the filter of our own times and individual decisions and struggles.

This book asks what spirituality and humility can possibly mean to us now and in this age. It leads us to recognize that the roots of integrity, of peace, lie in the earthiness, in the humus, that is our nature.

In this book, each of the steps of humility is examined from three vantage points: First, I ask myself how my attitude toward these steps evolved in my own understanding as a Benedictine, as a woman, as a seeker, over the years. It has not always been a salient or simple process.

Second, I take each step of humility off the page and explore the issues and questions implied in each of them here and now. To understand what the ancients were really addressing and why they were dealing with it as a central part of the spiritual life. It asks, Is union with God really possible?

What happens to individuality if a person is humble? How does something as questionable as humility change the quality of life for the seeker as well as for the world around us? It looks at the prerogatives and pitfalls of a false independence. It questions whether humility doesn't really suppress personal development. It looks for the difference between healthy pride and narcissism. It plumbs the place of human relationships in spiritual growth. It looks at the very modern questions that underlie the struggle with which each particular step of humility challenges us.

And finally, in the third segment of each chapter, I concentrate on the spiritual implications of humility for an individual's ultimate and empyreal growth. It brings the wisdom of the ages to bear on the struggles that come with trying to negotiate between the ways of the world and the ways of God today.

This book shines a light on the way to profound peace between us and the passions that drive us. It brings into focus the juices, the energy, the desires that, good as they are, augur to propel us into darkness. It sensitizes us to the impulses in need of gentling in ourselves if we are ever to become the light of God we are meant to be for others.

And always, it explores the place of humility in an individual person's spiritual life and the search for the fullness of personal human development.

It invites you to open up the dailiness of life and find God there. It invites you to become a "radical spirit," to put down your chains, to opt for a life that is free and authentic.

Indeed, the message of Zosimas rings on here: The chains we struggle with are the chains we have forged for ourselves.

They are the chasms of fear and contempt, the greed and arrogance, the hunger and emptiness we have yet to fill with the kinds of things that give our souls wings.

Or, to put it another way, welcome to the eternal search for the fullness of life.

*The First Step of Humility*

# RECOGNIZE THAT GOD IS GOD

The first step of humility, then, is that we keep "the fear—the reverence—of God always before our eyes (Ps. 36:2) and never forget it."

### *What is the challenge here?*

Humility has never been easy for me, at least not in the way it's written about in Chapter 7 of the Rule of Benedict.

I remember it all too well: It was 1952. I was a novice then, and preparation for full membership in the community was intense. Study, prayer, and almost total withdrawal from society marked that year as special, as different.

We didn't take college classes. Instead, we studied only the sixth-century Rule of Benedict, which formed the framework in which we would live out the rest of our lives. We not only prayed seven times a day but we studied the Latin in which the prayers were written in order to make those prayer periods understandable. Most of all, we concentrated on the Rule itself and, particularly, its cornerstone chapter, "Of Humility."

Every morning, in fact, we took an hour out of the day's regular duties—like baking altar breads or cleaning the chapel, washing windows or working in the kitchen—to study the Rule of Life under which we would soon promise to live. And that reading alone, not the manual labor, could well have been enough to make any thought of taking another step in the process impossible.

First, the Rule itself had been written fifteen centuries before this novitiate. Second, the book needed a good editor. Its language was for the most part musty and terse. And at least to a teenager in 1952, in a postwar era that had *new* and *liberating* written all over it, the ideas were chilling. One, in particular, drew my attention—and troubled me deeply: We were to "keep the fear of God always before our eyes and never forget it." Life was to be about "the fear of God"? Oh, great.

Years later, of course, they told us that "the fear of God" was now an archaic term, which meant "a mixed feeling of dread and reverence," but no one stressed the "reverence" of it in those days. "The fear of God" was the current translation, the defining essence of the relationship, and it stuck.

But I was young and new to monastic life, and the very language of this first step of humility was itself enough to be discouraging. What did it mean to "keep the fear of God always before our eyes"? I found the words stifling. Threatening, if truth were told. This God, it seemed, forever hovered over us just waiting for us to slip up. Then all heaven would pounce and, as the old Church manuals made so clear, close the gates of life to us forever. How could we possibly reverence a God like that, a God waiting in the dark, a specter in the night?

We were, I figured, entrapped by the presence of God, not liberated by it at all: This God sees "the thoughts of my heart," the chapter on humility put it. A discouraging thought in itself. We were condemned in that case just for thinking about something, before we even got a chance to try it. And yet, over the years, another light began to dawn: If that was true, then something else was surely just as true. This God who knew everything had to know, too, how hard I was trying to live decently, to love deeply, to grow beyond the gaps in my soul. And that, at least, was a calming thought.

But, there was something else that still bothered me: How was it even possible to claim to have nothing but God on my mind? How realistic could any of this be? My spirit sank. Did any of this chapter make sense? And if it did, would I ever be able to do it? I knew down deep that if the way this chapter read were really the way things were meant to be, I doubted that I would ever manage to get it right.

I simply could not imagine how to be perfectly immersed in God. Perfectly attuned to God. Perfectly satisfied with a life more intent on perfection than on life itself. I was looking for a spiritual life that was more grounded, more real, less ethereal. I wanted to move on, to find more of the sacred in life rather than cut it off in the name of Life. Something in me insisted that I needed to become fully human before I could even think of being perfectly holy. Why? Because striving to come to fullness is the nature of the human condition, and without that how can anyone be truly holy?

When I was younger, I didn't question that perfection was

possible. The truth, I learned as life went on, is that there is, indeed, always something lacking in us. We are not born perfect. The very process of human development—slow, stumbling, inquisitive, fickle all the way from infancy to old age—is proof of that. And I was living proof of that. I certainly did not become perfect as the years went by, however clear religion class had been about the process. I'm not even sure I wanted to be perfect if being afraid to try, to taste, to fail, and only then to try again was what it was all about. On the contrary, I seemed only to get further and further away from a spiritual ideal that felt to me like a living death. Every day, every new failure, left me less and less convinced that the ideal was even possible.

One situation in particular riled me every single day.

The prayer schedule provided for exercises in examination of conscience once at noon and again at night. Each of them concentrated on what we had done wrong that day. No one ever suggested that we might thank God for having helped us do anything right. So, I knelt in my pew, head down, and accused myself of things I considered too small, too meaningless, on which to waste my time. The Novice Directress, for instance, was particularly stressed by the fact that I walked too quickly, too loudly, on my leather soles in the hollow-sounding halls. Don't forget that one at examen time, I knew.

This "life of perfection" in a world of human imperfection was beginning to look like an excursion in neurosis. Surely the spiritual life was about more than walking heavily—a failing we were taught to confess weekly—along with dropping pins, spilling food, and making mistakes during community prayer. The boundaries between the moral, the immoral, and the amoral began to slip away, to blur, to become almost meaningless.

No, this great confrontation with God in the first step of humility had to be about more than making petty mistakes as we went about the routines of life. Clearly, the spiritual life had been reduced to a kind of psychosocial obsession someplace along the line. It was all about what we did and how. But what was that doing to the level of spirituality we were developing as a result? How could this possibly be the stuff of which sanctity was made?

If truth were known, every day of that regime I failed in more and more ways. Everything called "good" here was foreign to me. I spoke out of turn, ruminated incessantly, and broke silence repeatedly—which I learned quickly was a more reprehensible matter than the fact that what I was saying might be considered virtuous. So I said one thing in public and thought other things in private. I stayed on the path to religious life but spent a lot of time thinking about all the other paths I could have, and maybe should have, taken. I got smaller and smaller in my thinking, and my world got narrower as well. I felt like I was constantly underwater, my lungs bursting for want of breath, my heart stopped in midair. Most difficult of all, I was beginning to accept the fact that the "spiritual life" was a thing for spiritual children who counted childish things as its common currency.

"Love not your own will," the chapter on humility stressed. And I tried to stretch to those heights. But love what instead, then, I thought, in this place of puny pieties? "Our actions everywhere are in God's sight," the Rule reminded me, "and are reported by angels at every hour," looking for sins and vices.

The more I read, the more I felt trapped in the centrifuge of the self. I became a constant subject of my own smallness. Or, as a friend of mine told me years later, "I left the Church because if I stayed there I never could be anything but a failure."

What kind of spirituality was this? And what kind of God were we dealing with?

Where was the greatness of the spiritual life? Surely I had seen it once. In fact, I had tracked it in the wake of figures before us who had blazed an arc across the sky of life for all of us to follow.

Where, for instance, was the grand-heartedness of a Teresa of Avila, who had turned religious life upside down in her era—and sent my vision of it soaring in my own? Or a Martin of Tours, who refused to fight in the Roman imperial army in order to follow the peacemaker Jesus? Or a Joan of Arc, who argued conscience against the Church itself and had been willing to die for it? Or a Mother Catherine McAuley, who laid her life down to educate illiterate girls? Or a Mary Ward, who was condemned for trying to renew religious life outside of the spiritual architecture of her time but prevailed in the long run regardless? Or a Dorothy Day, who spent her life trying to recall the Church itself to the Gospel? These, and hundreds of others like them, had set my young soul on fire before I entered the monastery. But now here I was. This spiritual tradition, they told me, had lasted for over fifteen hundred years, yes. But was there anything left to it beyond the palest shadow of a guide to a kind of holiness crafted and gone dry in ages before? There had to be more to it than this equation of humility and spirituality with humiliation and repression.

I simply could not see in this chapter on humility a God great enough to follow.

Little by little I began to realize that it was not the spirituality of humility of which this chapter purports to speak that creates a problem. It was the notion of the kind of God to whom we owe homage that created the barriers. It was not the spirituality of humility that was my undoing. It was the image of God I had brought with me to the chapter that was my undoing.

But as the years went by, slowly but surely, the greater vision came back into focus. I finally uncovered the references to the psalms that this chapter on humility cited as its luminarias along the way to the expansion of the soul. The concern of the psalmists to whom Benedict's Rule points in this chapter is a God much bigger than the one forged by the popular notion of perfection. It is that God who eventually became the beacon and the rudder of life for me.

## What is the underlying issue?

If fear of God is the kernel and core of Benedictine humility, then the questions that must underlie our understanding it are these: Who is this God to whom we owe "fear, reverence, awe, genuflection"? How did Benedict of Nursia himself understand God? And, most of all, what does that say about the spiritual life in the Benedictine tradition, let alone to our own singular and often dispiriting journeys to God? And how shall we know if our concept of God and Benedict's concept of God are in sync?

One way to study the mind of Benedict—seldom marked, too often overlooked by modern readers of this ancient Rule— is to follow closely the Scripture passages Benedict draws on to give us a picture of God. Then there can be no misunderstanding about who it is to whom we owe both awe and homage. In fact, in this chapter Benedict chronicles God in action for us. He allows Scripture itself to explain this first step of humility by carefully citing the verses of the psalms that confirm his vision of God and the holy life.

Benedict's God is a defense from the storms of life, not a threat to human thriving (Ps. 7:10). This God sees *everything,* yes, which means that this God sees more than our weaknesses. This God sees, too, our needs, our pain, the struggle of being human (Ps. 38:10) and rewards those whose hearts are right and whose souls are righteous (Ps. 18:24). It is to this loving God, this merciful God, that we are to bring thankfulness, praise, veneration, awe—and genuflection (Ps. 50:21).

Clearly, to Benedict, God is a mighty God. This God knows what we are and stands with arms open to receive us—always and regardless. This is a poignant vision of God, a comforting one. This is a God who wants love, not fear, to be the bond between us. And real love, every lover knows, never goes away. Instead, it creates a kind of invisible but crystalline scrim toward which we are forever reaching out, however great the distance, to grasp the all of it.

Benedict is very clear about the character of God. This is a not a God of wrath, not a God who is indifferent to the world, not a ghoul of a God who spies on us in hope of watching us fall from grace. Most of all, this is not a "gotcha God" who simply lies in wait to punish us when we do. On the contrary.

In this light, God, the Doer of Magical Miracles outside the natural order, disappears. Instead, the God of Creation frees nature to take its course with us as we, too, test and taste and grow in wisdom, age, and grace. Having experienced life in all its glory, all its grief, we grow to the full height of our humanity. It is a slow process, yes, but in the end our choice for God is valid, is holy, because it is real, considered, not forced, not extorted. This God wants for creation the fullness of all the good that is in it.

Most of all, this caring God loves us and so refuses to interfere with our judgments or prevent our experiments with life. Instead, this God does us the respect of simply standing by, of being there to hold us up, of confirming our trust by leading us through the dim days and long nights. How else to explain the depth of soul of those who have survived great calamity, endured the brutal death of a child, struggled through crippling debilitation, torturous addictions, and yet come out of all of it praising the God who carried them through? Once we have known the strengthening presence of God in our own lives, we feel even closer to the God of Life after the tragedy than we did before it. No doubt about it: This God trusts humanity to work its own way to the fullness of its soulfulness.

Then the real miracle of Life—this right to choose our own destiny as well as the way we get there—with all its learnings, all our lessons, welcomes us home to new life and fresh understandings of God's way with God's creatures.

This first step of humility—this mandate "to keep the presence, the fear, the reverence, the awe of God always before our eyes . . . and never forget it"—does not crush us in the dust. Instead it makes us vulnerable to God. We are now accessible to the call of God. We are ready to live in the presence of God. We are open to the will of God both for each of us and for the world. God and God's will now stand to make an imprint in our lives.

Most important of all, this bald statement about the presence of God in our lives upends what the world knows as "merit theology." Benedict simply dismisses the whole idea that we are created to try to "merit" God. I remember only too well the number of novenas I counted in hope of good grades, the number of First Saturday masses I attended on free days to get out of purgatory after I died. I remember, too, the Friday night football game at which I pushed a hot dog out the other end of the bun till it fell to the ground below the viewing stands. The point was to avoid insulting the Protestant boy who took me there but at the same time to save my soul from the mortal sin of eating meat on Friday.

If I passed these do-or-die tests, this merit theology approach to God suggests, I would get God. If not, too bad.

The truth is that no one can merit God. We don't earn God a prayer, a legalistic hurdle, a devotion at a time. We don't need to earn God because the basic, life-giving truth is that we already have God. God is here. With us. Now. In this. Forever. What is important is for us to seek God—to come into touch with God—who is already seeking us. That is union with God. That is the marriage of two souls. Trying to earn God only keeps us Rule-centered failures, because no one can do it perfectly.

"To live in fear—in reverence—of God" attunes us to the presence of Life in life and renders us ready to detect its message in both good things and bad, in both simple things and difficult. It makes us bold enough to invite this God of Wonder to break us open to possibility and potential all our lives. It reminds us daily that the creation we see around us—electric in its energy, stolid in its eternal reproduction—has been created "for our weal and not our woe" as Scripture says (Jer. 29:11). So that we can grow in it and because of it. What more can life really be about? What should we fear in the face of a God who is, as the psalmist records in this Chapter of the Rule, our "shield, our defense"? What is there in the universe that can undo what the anchoring of ourselves to Life guarantees and God promises us through the psalmists?

This sense of awe for the God of a creation that is dynamic, ever-changing, always growing, this coming to know the God of possibility, frees us to trust life. Whatever happens to us now, this awareness that God is the center of everything makes anything and everything possible, makes anything and everything bearable. We know now that we are not in this alone. No, we cannot wrench life to our own designs because we did not create it and, therefore, cannot twist it to our schemes. We can, however, give it over to the God who is "Emmanuel"—who is indeed "God with us"—and so use this mundane present moment, too, to grow to full spiritual stature.

In the modern world, as we probe outer space and threaten to blow up the planet, the temptation to act like gods, even in our most personal, most private lives, is a common one. We have earned our arrogance: We have split the atom and plotted the human DNA. We have traveled faster than sound and made artificial hearts for babies. We are capable of feeding the globe and poisoning its land at the same time. The question is whether or not in the process we have smothered the basics of life: the awareness of what it really means to be human, to function humanely, to make humanity humane again.

No wonder then that in the chapter on humility, Benedict embeds a warning. He prompts us against the kind of pride that fails to pray that "God's will be done in us" and so warps the will of God for the world. He reminds us, as we go on remaking the world, of Scripture's warning: "There are ways which some call right that in the end plunge us into the depths of hell" (Prov. 16:25).

The lesson of this first degree of humility is that life well lived, life lived to the very height of our abilities, is life that pursues the will of God for the world.

The first step of humility, then, presents us with the problem of being able to distinguish pride from arrogance, humility from humiliation. Humility, ironically, is about coming to understand that spiritual simplicity is not about the debasement of the self. Nor is it about the aggrandizement of the self. So what is it?

### What are the spiritual implications of this step of humility?

Once upon a time, the ancients say, a disciple traveled far and wide to find a spiritual master who could lead him to the fullness of the spiritual life.

"What is it you seek?" the Holy One asked him.

"Master," the young seeker replied, "how can I ever be emancipated?"

The Zen Master answered: "You must ask yourself who it is who has put you in bondage."

The seeker is us. The missing spiritual master in this instance is the humility it takes to rest our lives in the consciousness that only God is God. Not us. And definitely not anything else in life that we have allowed to become our god rather than God.

The tendency to make shrines to ourselves, however, so easily becomes the norm of our existence. Our profession, our money, our social status, our need for public recognition begin to control us. Somewhere along the line we begin to sink into the routine, the system, ourselves. We settle down with the job, the family, the career path. And we grow inordinately blind to what rules us internally, or at least oblivious of our crying need for a spiritual center beyond ourselves. Yes, it's a natural phase in life, this exaltation of the ego. It is part and parcel of the process of human development, in fact. The only problem is that if and when we don't grow out of it, as we should, it renders us bereft of an adult spiritual life. We become, instead, spiritual infants, adolescents suspended halfway between maturity and self-indulgence. And then we wonder why our lives, full of everything, feel so empty.

As a result, we go through life dragging our chains behind us, trying to be what we are not, trying to do what can't be done, trying to elbow our way to the endless top of something. "I know more about ISIS than the generals," Donald Trump told the world. It was a display of false superiority that made people actually question his bid for the presidency of the United States. But such exaltation of the self tempts us all. It shatters the very internal peace we seek, and we don't have a clue why. Only when we are ready to admit that our chains of self-centeredness and hauteur are largely of our own construction are we ready to grow.

But the chains that bind us have many faces beyond raw arrogance. We chain ourselves to wealth that impoverishes our spirit. We give way to the sense of superiority that separates us from the rest of the human condition. And, most subtle of all, we lack a consciousness of the presence of God in life. It's then that we make ourselves the divinity within. And that message breeds the disease of privilege in us.

We tether ourselves to the part of ourselves that whispers in our ear that we can simply take what we do not have by right. We can take the lands of the poor for cash crops, for instance. We can steal just wages from women with impunity. We can destroy any one and any thing we label lesser than ourselves because of color, sex, race, or physical difference, for instance. We can make sex slaves out of little girls and submit animals to torture in the name of research. Worse, we can be indifferent to all those things because we are our only real agenda. We can make ourselves our own gods, for whom we require the awe of the rest of our world.

Chains such as these are forged in fear or resentment or pathological egotism, perhaps. But whatever they are, one thing is certain: The things that inflame our pettiness, our angers, our frustrations with our worlds hold us prisoners of ourselves. And that is exactly where humility comes in. It is in the first step of humility—this call to consciousness of the presence of God in life—that we can put down the burden of eternal self-aggrandizement, of unlimited power, of ceaseless demands, of unabated appetites.

God, humility teaches us then, is the part of my life that is really real. It is only the presence of God that will go on forever, that will not abandon me regardless of how often I fall and fail. Only when I acknowledge that I can relinquish my attempts, my self-proclaimed sovereign right, to shape the world to my own satisfaction, to wrench the world to my own designs, to gratify my unlimited desires, I can free myself from myself. I can give myself to something larger than myself. I can endure, as Shakespeare put it, "the slings and arrows of outrageous fortune" without collapse.

And I can survive. How? Because God is with us, holding us up, prodding us on, being the strength we now lack. It is that for which we genuflect. For that we are in awe.

This, then, is the ultimate moment of liberation. It comes with a flash of consciousness. This is union with God. Knowing—in our hearts now as well as in our minds—that God is truly "Emmanuel." This is what enables us to go into the dark places in life singing *Alleluia*. Nothing else.

Now we are ready to take risks we would surely otherwise avoid. Failure is not so frightening now, success not so captivating. Humility tells us that life is not all about us. What counts now is simply being in sync with the will of God for me, for the world. With that surrender goes the toxic effect of allowing my own will to obscure the good that is greater than I can see.

Most important of all, perhaps, all the childhood images of God—God the Magician, God the Santa Claus, God the wrathful Judge, God the Puppeteer—disappear. We know now that the God of Creation has shared power with us and remains with us to help us see life through. Our role is to do our part, to do our best, to trust the path. Our part is to become everything we are meant to be and so to make the world a better place because we have been here.

The first step toward liberation from the self is the acknowledgment that God is with us—first, last, and always—even in times of adversity. God, "our refuge and our strength," we've come to understand, can't be "merited," can't be earned, doesn't need to be won in some kind of ecclesial contest. No, this God is already with us. But when we truly, wholly, sincerely understand that, we are free to live life without the kind of fear that renders us powerless or sick with pride. Now we can live life with a relaxed grasp, doing what must be done, trusting the end to God. There is nothing to worry about, nothing to fear, once I decide to let God be God in my life.

The first step of humility frees us from the demon of merit theology, which forever marks us as failures. It frees us to grow through life always closer and closer to God. It reminds us always that God is not a goal to be achieved.

God is a presence to be recognized. Nor is God something that happens at the end of life. On the contrary, God is in every pore of it. This step of humility starts at the center, the core, the desired end of the spiritual life. It starts with the contemplation and consciousness of the Mystery that is the only reason, the only possibility of ever developing a truly spiritual life.

*The Second Step of Humility*

# KNOW THAT GOD'S WILL
# IS BEST FOR YOU

The second step of humility is that we "love not our own will nor take pleasure in the satisfaction of our desires . . . that we shall imitate by our actions that saying of Christ's: 'I have come not to do my own will, but the will of the One who sent me' (John 6:38)."

## What is the challenge here?

Every child in the Western world is raised to make independent decisions. I certainly was. One of my mother's earliest messages stays with me still: She said, after having been a young widow herself, "You have to be able to take care of yourself, Joan." Which meant: You have to know what you want and how to get it for yourself. . . . You have to be able to make your own decisions. Or more pointed still: You have to be independent. You need to be self-reliant. You need to make up your own mind.

So what does that have to do with living a spiritual life, I wondered, if we are to believe that being holy means giving up our own will? Are we really to submit our lives to strangers? And if so, what is holy about that? Who says their decisions will be better than ours? Or is this simply about power? About authority? About control?

When we were young sisters, every minute of our lives was in someone else's hands. What's more, there was no assurance whatsoever that we would ever again make the kinds of decisions other adults in the society—male seminarians included—took for granted. In fact, would we ever regain any significant control of our own lives? So what was spiritual about that? Or was it simply about being women who had been traditionally denied the right to make adult legal and economic decisions in any walk of life?

When the Twin Towers fell in New York City, on September 11, 2001, hundreds lost their lives because they listened to the announcement that told them to stay at their desks until further notice. And, at the same time, people lived that day because they did not obey that order. I had known for years that there was something wrong with the kind of obedience that denies human responsibility.

Years before that, I watched police and their dogs try to drive African Americans away from white lunch counters. I also saw a holy man, a religious prophet in our midst, lead thousands of peaceful people to defy the segregation laws that kept in civil chains a whole population who were brought here in physical chains against their will to begin with.

And on the other hand, a Navy SEAL, Derek Lovelace, died while in water training—hounded and dunked by his supervisor—while no one intervened because their orders were to complete the course themselves. And Lovelace died.

So, when is any of this holy and how do we know?

A child of this century, I found the second step of humility much less palatable, extremely less realistic than the first. To recognize that God is God, is one thing. To give up the only thing we have in common with God, free will, seemed to me to be entirely another. What was the sense, the purpose of such a thing? What's more, my entire world confirmed the question.

After all, if an American birthright is anything, it is a charter for self-will. If the West models anything about relationships, it is that they must be framed with the expectation of equality, independence, and sovereignty. If representative government has any goal whatsoever, it is the search for the common will that emerges out of the shaping and polishing of a bevy of individual wills painfully knitted into one. No, giving up our individual wills is not the ideal human response of Western society. Nor, in a sense, I had thought since I was six years old, should it be.

My life, in other words, was a long way from the sixth-century Italian culture that had spawned a spirituality based on humility. I could understand its place there, perhaps. But here? In my world?

I struggled with the whole concept—most of all, perhaps—philosophically. Autonomous human beings, unfettered and unaware of their limitations, can be a dangerous species, of course. But history also tells another story, and history was not on the side of control, it seemed. On the contrary.

The commitment of a strong-willed person is a public bulwark against tyranny, against autocracy, against the multiple and regular onslaughts on political freedom. Because of their insight, their courage, their fully focused resistance to public decisions made without their input or their response, a few of them have saved many of us.

Strong individuals freed slaves. They enfranchised women. They fought for civil rights, for the protection of children, for justice at polling places, for just wages and medical care for the poorest of the poor. They became the backbone of the nation. They dug out the scandal of the sexual abuse of children with their bare hands. And in our time, they insist on the protection of the poor, the elderly, and the refugees. They struggle to hold the Union together while they pursue the rights of the minorities everywhere. They are living signs of the virtue of free will.

To be told that for any reason whatsoever, then, it is good to put down self-will is, in the modern world, an anomaly. I know the feeling.

Where I came from, even elementary school children were taught independence, but in consort with obedience, a kind of moral schizophrenia if I ever saw it. To even think of attempting to live both ideals at the same time had all the earmarks of a collision course with life. So, which comes first? Obedience or self-direction?

The tension between those two polar conceptions of the perfect life emerged early in the process of my spiritual development. The whole context became a backdrop for another kind of spiritual struggle. And I felt it keenly.

The spiritual life, after all, was made up of constraints,

and religious life was organized to institutionalize every one of them. It was holy to be "humble"—meaning docile and unquestioning. It was saintly to be pious—meaning devoted to being perfect as someone else had defined perfection. It was the essence of humility to be selfless—meaning largely invisible, quiet, retiring, and not inclined to take up too much public space.

I remember that when I announced I had decided to enter the monastic life within the next couple of months, my mother's comment was "Just remember, Joan, if you go there they will not allow you to lie down with your feet up on the sofa again like you do here." I was embarrassed by what I considered the triviality of such a response to so exalted a decision. Years later, I understood what she meant—and she was right. Somewhere along the line, sofas had gotten mixed up with other, more sublime measures of sanctity. As in, was never putting my feet up on a sofa again a proper measure of real obedience, real sanctity, or not?

As the years went by, the question became more universal, more important. Sofas became sofas again, neither a standard of sanctity nor a rule in a rule book. That kind of sacred metric, like hats for girls in church, disappeared in the light of more important issues. Just exactly what sanctity was all about in a world where 65 million refugees shuffled from one border to the next—tired, hungry, abandoned, and abused—became a more real test of moral meaning than sofas would ever be again.

The question of the surrender of self-will, however, is really no easier to answer now than it was then, but the answers have grown more substantive at least. More adult. More worth committing a life to than the mere notion that if something is painful, it must be holy-making.

My own personal problem with this second step of humility lay in the struggle to determine when and under what conditions anyone ought to even think of surrendering self-will. More than that, how can such an abdication of self-direction ever possibly be holy? And what kind of humility, I wondered all those years ago, were they talking about: abnegation for its own sake, spinelessness as a synonym for holiness, submission as a sign of conversion? Was this break-a-person-down time? And if so, for whose sake, for what good?

I began to draw some lines in my head: For instance, some clarity, both spiritual and emotional, is in order. First, negation for its own sake is not holiness, I decided. It's simply harassment of the soul designed to make discomfort or neediness spiritually good for their own sakes. It puts the focus on nonessentials, where the focus does not belong. It emphasizes one virtue—detachment or penance—at the expense of multiple others, like prophetic witness and reckless generosity, voluntary poverty and selfless ministry to a wounded world.

Surely, I decided, negation has little or nothing to do with either humility or the constraint of an errant will. It can easily encourage us to hide behind the trappings of false holiness rather than actually do what holiness demands.

Spinelessness, the adulation of weakness in the face of evil when strength is what's required, only makes a person more interested in social approval than in following Jesus. The inability to speak up for the truth, for justice, for the end of social corruption is not humility. It is, at best, a mask that hides our inability either to make a decision or to take a stand in the face of sin.

Or worse, the willingness to submit to superiors on issues either unjust or meaningless only masks a disingenuous—a false—capitulation of personal responsibility.

Point: Control, invisibility, and silencing under the hubris of humility reduce the adult to the level of spiritual childhood and calls that holy. There is no humility in allowing anyone to take away my need to claim my own conscience. I was there, so I'm sure of that. I was slow at coming to protest the Vietnam War. I was slow at speaking out about segregation and racism. I was slow at being honest enough to say that the Church's position on women is wrong. Clearly, I had learned to obey, but I had not learned, as this Chapter of the Rule reminded me, to do "the will of the One who sent me" (John 6:38).

Indeed, a number of things mask as humility that are at best ways to gain favor, save my circle of friends, keep public approval. It's here, I learned over the years, that the second step of humility comes to free us from the smallest part of ourselves.

I am still learning, of course, but at least now I have a better picture of what it would look like to be truly humble.

## What is the underlying issue?

The monks of the third- and fourth-century Egyptian desert were known for the spiritual guidance they shared with one another. In addition, thousands of laity trekked out to their simple cells in search of spiritual advice. Of the sayings collected by these avid disciples, one stands out for its insight into the second step of humility. "A brother asked Abba Poemen," they say, "How ought we to act in the place where we dwell?" And Abba Poemen answered: "Show discretion towards a stranger; show respect to the Elders; do not impose your own point of view, then, you will live in peace."

According to Abba Poemen, obviously, the issue is how "to act in the place where we dwell." And the answer is clear: Do the will of God. But how to know what that is eludes us.

The thinking upon which the second step of humility rests is fascinating. The second step says, "Do not love your own will . . ." It does not say, Do not have one. On the contrary. We must learn young not to be afraid to think separately from those around us. In fact, our own interpretation of the way our piece of the world goes round is actually our gift to it. Only when we have at our disposal all the possible ways of reading any situation can we begin to assess its effects, let alone fashion its future possibilities. And that, in fact, is where God's will emerges.

Abba Poemen's saying enables us to do it all. He tells us to show attention even to strangers. He wants us to listen to other people, no matter how foreign. He wants us to open our minds to new and fresh ideas. He wants us to attribute wisdom—discretion—to everyone, for fear we stunt our own spiritual growth by failing to attend to the judgments of others.

He wants us, too, to show respect to the elders—to those who endured the heat of the noonday sun long years before us and so formed the world we're living in now. Clearly, he wants us to realize that we did not invent the wheel. It came from the hands of others—generations ago. Before deciding to change it now, he cautions us to understand why they did what they did then as well as what they think we ourselves ought to be doing now.

The counsel of the ages is clear. As the seventeenth-century Japanese poet Bashō says, "I do not seek to follow in the footsteps of the men of old; I seek what they sought." In that practice lies our respect for those who have gone before us. It is not that we must continue what they did, for those ideas or customs may have long ago dimmed. But we must respect their vision, their efforts, their values, their ideals, their perseverance, their gift to yesterday that makes today possible. To those who would destroy everything that went before them, humility damps the urge. Only by standing on the shoulders of the past can we begin to see the amount of perseverance it takes to do the will of God for the world; in fact, to do anything of value for the world.

Then Abba Poemen shows us all what the end of the teaching implies: "Do not impose your own point of view, then, you will live in peace."

The real issue, then, is this: Of course the second step of humility follows from the first. If we love God above all else, we shall certainly love God's will above all else. But where does God's will really come from, and how can we recognize it?

The answer, Abba Poemen thinks, is very simple, very straightforward. We discover the will of God, he intimates, by collecting all the wisdom we can—past and present—and then making good judgments ourselves. Which point of view, we must then ask ourselves, comes closest to God's loving will for the world now and here? Which point of view brings justice and equality, peace and possibility to the world at large? If not now, certainly in times to come.

The issue under the need to do the will of God is what it means to choose human community in the face of rampant and rapacious individualism.

This second step of humility moves us out of ourselves in order to appreciate the insights, see the needs, respect the values, and honor the wisdom of the whole world.

It tells us to listen to everyone in the family, to the lowest workers on the totem pole, to the multiple needs of a pluralistic society. And then to proceed accordingly.

It is a straight line from the mind of God to the needs of the world. With need as our filter, the will of God for the world cannot possibly be difficult to determine. When children are starving around the world, the systems that permit such a thing, enable such oppression, in fact, must surely be confronted. And changed. Authority must never trump justice.

The first step of humility is about internalizing the presence of God. The second follows from the first: The presence of God requires our response. God is not a thought now. No, now, given the second step of humility, God is a way of thinking. We are not just talking about the God of Love now. Now we are beginning to talk about what it means to love God.

Submission to the will of God, of course, requires that I finally learn to relinquish my rabid devotion to self-will. The entire world, the whole universe, is the treasure house of the will of God, the mind of God for us all. It means that when I find myself liking my ideas and my plans better than others, struggling to impose them, cutting people off in conversation before they can even lay out all of their ideas, the caution light will go on in my heart. I will then begin to think again—only this time I will be thinking about everybody else's ideas and answers, plans and visions, needs and hopes for life. Not simply my own.

This is the change point of life. This is where humility becomes a way of life rather than a threat to personal ambition and ability. I am beginning to understand now that there are ways of doing things other than my own. There are other answers to the question that are more inclusive of the effects of this moment on others—"down to the seventh generation"—as the Native Americans teach. I begin to realize that there are other plans to consider first, rather than my own. Now, by listening to others, I begin to understand the meaning of "discernment" and, led by the Spirit, I come to peace.

At this point, I begin to see the world through the eyes and the mind of God. All life is God's will, not simply mine. All peoples are the image of God, not only my kind. All of us have something to say, and in listening to the insights of others, we each get closer to the mind of God. Contemplation of the will of God for us all is the spiritual work of a lifetime, the purpose of life. Otherwise, how can I ever be sure that I am really following the will of the God whose will is therefore everywhere and in everyone else, as well?

Then peace comes. Why? Because then we are in contention with no one. We aren't arm wrestling with anyone. We are simply part of the gathering of ideas that will someday serve to make the world a better place. In our time? Possibly not. By me? Seldom. Because of me? Undoubtedly.

The first and second steps of humility are the path to right-heartedness in life, to life lived between the actual and the spiritual. The desert monastic Isaac the Syrian spoke about it in the seventh century, and his ancient insights get truer by the day. Isaac says, "Knowledge of God and knowledge of self give birth to humility." When I know who God is—and accept that glory, that ultimacy—then I know who I am. And who I am not. And I am not God. But I am "made in the image of God" in order to mirror God here.

That God's will is better for me than my own stumbling attempts to pretend to be more than I am becomes obvious. Isaac was right: It is knowing our place in the universe that makes for humility, that guarantees us peace. And we are neither its glory nor its ultimacy. That puts a lot of things into a more proper perspective, doesn't it?

*What are the spiritual implications of this step of humility?*

The popular images of the presence of God in life are stern ones. Forbidding ones. They speak of mistrust and punishment, of rules and sins, of dread and control. God the Policeman, God the Disciplinarian, God the Spy are all more common in the common mind than is the tender, caring God, the Good Shepherd. We have all grown up with too many of the control images. But not here. Not in Benedictine spirituality.

Here, in the very first two steps of humility, all of those ideas of God the Master Rule Giver, God the Autocrat evaporate. Here God becomes our perpetually present Lover—Mother, Father, Refuge—whose will for us is shalom, peace. This is the God who created us—and knows us.

Not even the Ten Commandments assume the extinction

of our human errors. That is impossible in the realm of the human. No, it is rather a belief in the possibility of human growth, your growth and mine, particular to each of us but universal to all of us, nevertheless.

The presence of God is not about our being under suspicion and disbelief. On the contrary. The commandments themselves are all about right relationships. Their subject matter is manifest: Love God, love your family, love your neighbor, love well, do not seek satisfaction in amassing what is not yours. But most apparent of all, one message rings through every one of them: The will of God for the world—peace and justice—is all you need. When the will of God for the world finally comes, you will have what you need, what you yourself have been seeking all your life. The only bewilderment, perhaps, lies in the fact that we ourselves must be part of bringing the will of God.

These first two steps of humility repeat the mandate to trust our trustworthy God. They gear us to love rather than fear our loving God, to put down our own will for dominance, so that the will of God for the common good might come. In this simple model lies the peace of God.

The spiritual implications of such a life are plain. We cannot capture God. No amount of pious record keeping—a rosary a day, Sunday church attendance, so much tithing, or yoga, or meditation, or *minyans*—can guarantee us depth and authenticity in the spiritual life. Only this merging of two wills— God's and mine—cements the human-divine relationship.

Humility is the virtue of liberation from the tyranny of the self. Now we have bigger things to be about in life than personal aggrandizement. The humble, no matter how great, do not spend their lives intent on controlling the rest of their tiny little worlds. On the contrary. Once we learn to let God be God, once we accept the fact that the will of God is greater, broader, deeper, more loving than our own, we are content to learn from others. We begin to see everyone around us as a lesson in living. We find ourselves stretched to honor the gifts of others as well as the value of our own.

To become open to the rest of the world, to people of other colors, to countries with other customs, to the devout of other religious traditions is the spiritual gold standard of inclusiveness. It says without doubt that I have finally accepted that I am no longer the center of the universe. Conversely, at this point I see that my God is also the God of the universe. I have come to realize that if, indeed, there is only one God, then the message of that God to the rest of the world must be the same as God's will for me and mine. The well-being that God seeks for me is likewise sought for all others. How can I not speak for their needs, see their values, argue for their rights, work to support their children?

Most of all, perhaps, humility frees me from the need to wrestle life to my own designs. My public goal now is not to make others just like me. It is to see that my goals are no obstacles to theirs as they strive to achieve their own share of the gifts of God.

My clear obligation now is to see that God's will for people everywhere is not being deliberately thwarted, not being ignored in favor of our own. How can we enslave a people to make our shoes and our children's toys and our clothes in sweatshops across the world? How can we agree to buy without protest foreign imports that pay their makers—often children under twelve years old—$0.70 a day to send us what we will sell here for $125.00? How can we allow the genetic manipulation of seeds that cannot reproduce so that we become the food basket of the world as well as the arms merchant of the world? How can we count our will to power and wealth a greater good than others' will for a decent life? And how can we call ourselves humble—spiritual—if we do?

Equally critical to my own spiritual depth, perhaps, is the fact that in these first two steps of humility is the spiritual lesson that gives emotional stability to life. They enable me to accept unplanned change with dogged, steadfast equanimity, with imperturbable faith. If God is God and I have learned to trust the God of Surprises, there is little now that can really rock, convulse, or upend my emotional ground. I learn to expect the unexpected. More than that, I learn to expect that, in the end, this moment of change, however devastating, will be to my good.

Finally, I learn from these two steps of humility what religion seldom teaches: that being sinless is not enough. It's being steeped in the mind of God that is important. It's coming to see the world as God sees the world that changes things. It's giving my life so that the mind of God for the world might actually become the way of life for the world. It's about spending my life so that the reign of God might come.

In these first two steps of humility, we ground ourselves in God. We learn to sing new songs in life. We sing *Alleluia* now—God is with us—whatever the circumstances, whatever the outcome.

We sing full-throated with the poet Gerard Manley Hopkins, "The world is charged with the grandeur of God." And finally we sing with the psalmist: "Oh, God. It is you for whom I long throughout the day" (Ps. 63:1).

Unless we can grasp the idea that doing the will of God is greater for my own peace of mind than doing my own will, we stand to find life a cramping, barren, and unloving place.

But if and when doing the will of God becomes the compass point of my life, no amount of effort toward it can ever be too much, no road to its accomplishment too long.

The demon that masters me is the arrogance of self-development. The second step of humility frees me to realize that life's singular purpose is becoming what I was created to be—co-creators with the God of Life. Now I am free to grow bigger than my focus on my small self would ever otherwise allow.

*The Third Step of Humility*

# SEEK DIRECTION FROM
# WISDOM FIGURES

The third step of humility is that "we submit to the prioress or abbot in all obedience for the love of God."

## *What is the challenge here?*

I look back sometimes and wonder whether, if I had read the Rule of Benedict before I entered, I would ever have entered religious life at all. The ideas in it were simply foreign to my time and place. They came from a planet with which I had had no experience and even less understanding. "Fear" God, or in some versions "Reverence" God, it said—whatever that meant in an era when keeping the rules was what really mattered, more than developing a consciousness of the presence of God. Give up your own will, it went on. And now, worst of all, it said we were to "submit . . . in all obedience" to whoever was the authority figure of the time. I remember my first taste of it all. It was the summer I entered and I had been told to come to the convent to talk to the prioress about the high school courses I would still need to take.

She rattled them off in good order. "Now let's see, this year you will take American history, English, chemistry, physics, French . . ." and then I said, "Not French, Spanish." But she persisted. "Oh no, my dear," she said. "You will take American history, English, chemistry, physics, and French." I persisted, too. "But, Mother," I said, "I don't like French. I like Spanish." She raised her eyebrows a bit and said—first convent lesson coming up—"My dear child, we don't say we don't like anything." And I said, incredulous and quick to correct the situation, "Do we lie?"

The lines had already been drawn. Life, from now on, was not a personal decision; it was a communal process.

In the first two steps toward humility, Benedictine spirituality deals with the questions Who is God? and What does it mean to do the will of God? Then, here in the third step, the real struggle with the personal pursuit of humility really begins. Here, we are told, it seems, that obedience is to be preferred to either creativity or intelligence.

Maybe it's the word *submit* that rankled. Early on, I could hear overtones of conquest here, hints of degradation. My soul shuddered at the very thought of accepting surrender—even as an exercise in humility. If humility is a kind of orchestrated weakness, I thought, how can it possibly be anything real? Let alone do anything good for the psyche, anything healthy for the soul.

Trust me: It can take years to separate real humility from the practice of humiliation. But it doesn't take too long to figure out that they are not the same thing. Small children caught talking in school and made to wear long, ugly paper tongues around their necks for the rest of the day know the difference. Is it punishment? Indeed. Is it psychologically transformative?

Almost never. That kind of treatment, at most, sets up the kind of fear and resistance that act out later, in other places and in other ways.

The truth is that something feels wrong about setting up a human being, let alone an adult, to kowtow, to acquiesce, to surrender. Then to call that spirituality, or even piety, let alone virtue—obedience—is simply distasteful. American sailors on their knees, hands behind their heads, that's surrender. That's not virtue. The control of women by men in the name of marriage is not love, that's abasement. The verbal denunciations of gays, blacks, women, minorities in coarse and vulgar language is not freedom of speech, it's degradation. And none of those things lead to humility; they lead to anger, to ignominy, to war. Not to the love of God.

Most of all, it seemed to me to be play-school humility. The so-called humility that pretends a submission that does not, should not, be required of any adult, is an unseemly indicator for a relationship between equals. The whole idea smacks of indignity, a lack of respect for another human being. Roman society, the society for which this step of humility was first written, was a highly stratified one: Romans on top, foreigners and slaves on the bottom. To call the mighty to such a low state might well have been a great equalizer then, but now? Among equals?

I simply could not understand how the kind of humility that requires capitulation from anyone could possibly apply to a spiritual state. And if it did, what kind of a life could that possibly be in our time? In a time that boasts that its ideal is personal freedom and political equality? And more than that, to a religious society whose theology says of itself, "We—human beings—are made slightly lower than the angels"?

There had to be something wrong with that kind of humility. And there is. That kind of humility is not humility at all. It is the defacement of the face of God in the other. It wants submission rather than growth. It wants compliance where commitment to another whole attitude toward life must develop instead.

What's wrong with it, I came to understand over the years, is that "humility"—invisibility—of that ilk is imposed. There is nothing free about it and so there is nothing real about it. It is a game played by the powerful on the powerless to demonstrate superiority. And people who comply with such a charade erase themselves from the responsible part of the human race.

For years I accepted the idea that such invisibility, both personal and psychological, was simply part of the kind of asceticism that real religious fervor required. It had something to do with effacement of the self. Its purpose was the kind of obedience to the will of God that the first and second steps of humility implied. But was getting permission from a superior to walk over to a parish school I'd been ordered to teach in—as we were expected to do monthly—really the serious content of the vow of obedience I'd taken? Or, even now, is treating undocumented refugees like pawns rather than as human beings really "Christian"?

For me there were questions all along the way about this

concept of obedience that never quite went away, all of them compounded by a rising consciousness of the oppression of women in society. Except for one problem. This Rule had originally been written by a man for men. For Roman men—with all the assumptions of independence their status in society implied. There had to be more to it than simply the oppression of women. It had to have something to do with the development of the spiritual life itself, female or male. And to be real humility—whatever that was—it had to have something to do with cultivating a relationship with the loving, caring, life-expanding God of the first and second steps of humility.

Suddenly I knew the problem: How could I say that I really believed the will of God was best for me if I refused to accept the fact that the will of others could be good for me, too? It was the spiritual conundrum of all time. How is it that the growth of my own soul lies in its relationship to the plans of others?

Then, a light in my soul went on: Learning to defer to those who were entrusted with the chrysalises of our lives has more to do with growth than with repression. Voluntary deference is about learning to see the place of others in our lives as necessary to the ripening of our own.

For me, the examples came quick and sure over the years: I would never have chosen to teach grade school if I had been making my own decisions. But it was four years of grade schoolers whose questions and false starts and open hearts taught me how to teach.

I would never have tried to teach high school after being crippled by polio for fear I would not be able to connect with older students. But it was those very limitations and the very physical help I got from them during that period that brought me back to full strength in both body and personality.

I would never have been a writer if my life had not taken the twists and turns that being part of community life demanded. What I loved to do—but fully expected never to be able to do—began because others put me in positions that required it.

Out of this braiding of relationships would come a lot of other things that had to be dealt with, of course: frustration, sometimes; impatience, often; even resistance, at times. But it was learning to deal well with others—and to survive despite the fact that it all seemed to be too much—that would put me in touch with the wisdom of the universe. We are all meant, I learned at long last, to work it out together. We are all meant to learn to listen to one another. Over and over again.

So here, in these interactions with the equally powerful independence of others, would come the limiting, the stretching, of my own. It was that obedience, that learning to listen to visions of life quite different from my own, that would test and try my respect for the God-life that lives in others as well as in me.

It also requires that I learn to trust that others have my good in mind as much as I do. Aye, there's the rub: Psychologists long ago developed the Trust Test in an attempt to convince their clients that whatever bad happened they could expect help enough to save them from the worst of it.

So they put people in two circles, one behind the other. At a signal known only to those in the front line, client one fell backward. The person behind client one was meant to stop the fall, despite the fact that she or he did not know when it would happen. One person, in other words, had to trust that someone would catch her before she hurt herself in the free fall. The other person had to stay alert to the needs of the first.

The challenge of the Trust Test is as important for the soul as it is for the body: To discover that you can be caught in free fall by the vision, the advice, the care of a perfect stranger makes every day of life a safer, happier, and more meaningful one. It may also be the greatest spiritual lesson we ever learn.

Humility is the willingness to trust ourselves to the universe, to the people in our lives, to the wisdom of others. We are told to relinquish our self-centeredness to the universal will, to realize that we are attuned to one another and that the others are at least as wise and caring as we are.

The God who made us has provided for us. We know that because behind us is the God who supports us always. However many times we fail. However many times we fall. However much the ground under our most unstable and fragile selves gives way.

## What is the underlying issue?

The third step of humility asks the obvious, the overriding question, the question that must be dealt with by all people at all times and everywhere. The question is incontrovertible: What is obedience? Really. And what does obedience have to do with humility? And what does humility have to do with freedom and authenticity?

The question is not an easy one to answer. Most definitions of *obedience,* scholars tell us, have been corrupted to such a degree that its original meaning is hardly salvageable anymore.

The contemporary answer is that the word *obedience* itself emerged in the thirteenth century from a Latin word meaning "to listen." Repeat: to listen. Not to kowtow. Not to capitulate. Only later, in a climate of courts and courtiers, did it begin to mean "bow down," curtsy or genuflect. Nowhere in any etymology text is *obedience* translated as "to jump on command." To grovel. To defer. To relinquish all judgment in the process. On the contrary. Those words came out of submission to ruling powers, to ecclesiastical figures, to symbols of power in the secular world. They were not of the language of God.

The very etymology of the word digs down into the soul, gives layers of new meaning to notions of adult obedience and the relationship of the soul to God.

In fact, obedience, listening, is a very freeing concept. The call to listen is everywhere in Scripture where the conflict of one power with another threatens to tip the scales of humanity toward the powers of this world. Then we must choose. When what makes us human—the power to think, to decide, to comply—does not make us holy, then we have an obedience problem. Then obedience demands that we disobey, that we listen to a higher law. Or to put it another way, the thousands of men and women arrested for protesting war, segregation, fossil fuels, the abuse of children, animal research programs, and every kind of social injustice everywhere are obeying a basic call to become fully developed human beings. They are listening to the needs of the world around them and obeying these calls for justice.

Scripture is full of models of those who think of themselves as the absolute power but spend no time whatsoever listening to the very people their exalted positions require them to hear. And they are legion—all the way from the prophets of Israel whom the authorities rejected to Jesus before Herod, who condemned him to die. Whenever power and justice conflict, power must give way.

In fact, disobedience has a glorious history; there is a long line of holy dissidents who said no when no was the only holy answer.

In the Acts of the Apostles, Peter and John stand before the Council of Jerusalem because by proclaiming the teachings of Jesus they had defied the council's orders. They remained steadfast in the certainty that this command was without divine merit. Peter and the other apostles replied in the face of imprisonment: "We must obey God rather than human beings!"

Holy defiance is not peculiar to a few anecdotal incidents. Instead, this choice of the will of God over the laws of the land is an ancient witness not a new one, where the search for God is concerned. In Exodus the midwives Shiphrah and Puah refuse to obey the Egyptian Pharaoh and murder the newborn boys of the Israelites. Later, Esther and Mordecai plot together to rescue the Jewish people despite the fact that they had been sentenced to death by the King's counselor. Jeremiah faces a death sentence for continuing to preach the Word of God.

Most significant of all, perhaps, is that, of the 613 laws in the Torah, Chief Rabbi Jonathan Sacks points out, not one uses the word *obey*. God, the rabbi says, does not impose the intractable on Israel. God uses the word *shema*. Attend to. Take seriously. Pay attention. Listen to me, O Israel.

The point is transparent: God invites the people of Israel to understanding, to attention, to consideration, to contemplation of the will of God for all their lives.

And so it is true for us as well.

This third step of humility invites us to learn to give up the kind of power that pits us against the will of God for us. By listening to our elders, our guides, our directors, whose models of the will of God are models for us, we begin the road to conversion of the selfish self. We forgo arrogance and our sense of personal omnipotence. We open ourselves to the wisdom of others, to living examples of the will of God, and so begin to embrace the wisdom of humility ourselves.

Humility does not necessarily require me to agree and comply with everyone else's position, but it does demand that I be willing to understand and respect the many sides of every issue. It does demand that I recognize that the positions of authority figures which are not in conflict with the will of God may also reflect the will of God for me. At the same time, it requires me to speak up for my own interpretations of what the will of God demands here and now. It takes humility to understand that there are multiple approaches to every question. And in the end, it takes humility to choose the path that is the straightest route to the will of God for me.

The third step of humility calls us to live our lives, not by bowing down to the law—any law—but by following the star that is above the law. By giving our lives to the law of God, whatever the cost, we make God the center, the lodestone of our lives.

Just because human beings so often dress themselves in the trappings of power does not give them power over either our consciences or our souls. Our obeisance rests always with our obligation to follow the One who has the ultimate right to say to us, "Listen. Pay attention to what I am telling you. Heed my will."

The list of those who model total attention to the will of God for the world is legion: the martyrs of the early Church, the prophets of ancient Israel, the great saints who resisted the temptation to please the system rather than do the will of God. And countless numbers of them in our own time and world: Thomas Merton, the monks of Tibhirine, the women martyrs of El Salvador, Martin Luther King, Jr., Dietrich Bonhoeffer, Franz Jägerstätter, Dorothy Day, Mahatma Gandhi—all confronted the demands of obeisance to personal power with obedience to the law of God. When we are ready to do the same, when we are willing first to listen to the voice of God deep within us—then and only then can we be sure that we are beginning to understand that our relationship to God depends on the humility it takes to choose right over power—whatever the price to be paid for doing it.

The fact is that our lives are full of guides, formal and informal, authoritative and not, holy and also committed to the will of God. They lead us always to choose the best rather than the better, the great rather than the good, the just over the unjust. The will of God over the ways of the world.

Most of all, it is humility that frees me from becoming enslaved to power, to deference for its own sake. Yet, at the same time, the willingness to be led by others becomes a sign that I am aware of my own limitations. By the way, remember the prioress who was setting up my academic courses for the year? Just as the Rule requires, she listened "to the younger"—to me—as well as to the older members of the community, an obvious accommodation of age to youth—not a negotiated solution at all. So I took Spanish rather than French that year and, incidentally, the model of her humility has made all the difference in my life.

The only question, then, is, What does humility have to do with your spiritual life and mine? Today, in a world of great powers and invisible peoples, of more answers than questions, what does obedience demand of us and where does it lie?

*What are the spiritual implications of this step of humility?*

The short answer? Easy: The way we define obedience shapes the way we live out what we know to be the call of the spiritual life.

The way I develop as a human being and the way I develop as a spiritual person are not totally unlike.

In terms of human development, the search for security is basic. We spend years assessing the environment to determine what we need to do to fit into it. Finally, we manage, bit by bit, to chart our own route through life.

Sometimes we shape it; sometimes it shapes us. The process is a long and complex one.

But the development of the spiritual life has some basics, too. First, we learn what kind of God, God is—a loving Presence or a rigid Judge. Most important of all, we learn the rules our spiritual tradition uses to direct us through life and give us some criteria along the way.

But, as we grow into the rules, we also grow out of them.

We test them and stretch them, and sometimes abandon them entirely. Until, finally, a belief system emerges.

Eventually, out of the angst and anxiety of envisioning a life equal to the God we've drawn for ourselves—Judge, Jailer, Magician, Puppeteer, Creator, Lover, Presence—we either grow spiritually mature or languish in spiritual childhood all our lives.

The whole cycle is a life-changing process. But it takes years to understand obedience itself. The struggle to determine to what and to whom we owe obedience is a fundamental part of the development of both a spiritual life and a totally mature human life.

The meaning we give to *obedience* is, in the end, the measure of the fullness of our spiritual development. And humility is its cornerstone.

The struggle with obedience is a natural part of every human system—family, church, government, work. It starts when a toddler says the first "No!" and ends only when life ends. The need to define the place and nature of authority is the universal call to holiness.

Indeed, authority and obedience are human conditions that must be resolved, that can't be ignored, because the very foundations of every relationship, every institution, and even the character of civilization itself depend on it. The Bishop-Pastor of the first high school I taught in, for instance, asked every new young sister sent to his school one question: "Sister," he said, "what will you do if a fire starts in the school?" And if the young sister said "Tell the superior" instead of "Pull the fire alarm" she was sent back to Erie to seek another position.

It is, after all, authority and the kind of obedience that accompanies it that brings order and purpose, compliance or character to a situation. It denies chaos the right to reign over us and brings direction to everything we do in life. But to what are we aiming? And for what? And with what effects? The questions are devastatingly complex, confusing, fairly shimmering with uncertainty. And worse, on the answers to such questions hinges the contract we call society.

The fact is that obedience brings with it two very different possibilities: Obedience at its worst stands to entrap us for its own sake. On the other hand, obedience just as often functions to unleash us. Both aspects have profound social consequences. One of the functions of spiritual maturity is to enable us to tell one from the other.

One of this era's most important, most telling, pieces of social research relates directly to what Benedictine spirituality calls the third step of humility, the notion that we are to submit to superiors "in all obedience for the love of God." The experiment, first conducted in 1961 by Yale social psychologist Stanley Milgram, exposed a dimension of obedience seldom questioned before, but is absolutely key to the spiritual life.

The key to understanding findings such as these is the awareness that the experimenters in the project had an authority founded in expertise. "I did it," many explained after the experiment was over, "because I thought they were doctors." Or, in other cases, "because they knew what they were doing and I didn't."

The findings of the Milgram study exposed the fact that people are likely to obey authority figures without question.

When commanded by "authorities," this time professors and assistants in white lab coats carrying clipboards, from 61 to 66 percent of the participants willingly administered what would have been fatal "shock treatments" to those they were told had failed to respond to the test protocol "correctly." Just as important, perhaps, Milgram himself said later, the participants who had themselves refused to administer the final shocks, nevertheless did not demand that the experiment be discontinued.

At a time when society was grappling with the question of how it was that ordinary, decent, good people had cooperated at one level or another with the Nazi genocide of over 6 million Jews, homosexuals, and gypsies, these findings were deeply problematic. They raised the specter that obedience itself can be dangerous—both when we obey and when we don't. The simple fact that someone gives us an order, the Nuremburg war crimes tribunals held, does not free us from moral responsibility for the effect of the action.

The temptation is to dismiss the Nuremberg decision as an indication only of an aberration in history. And yet, there is more than enough evidence in society to signal just how willing we all are to hand over our conscience to others.

In the detention camp at Guantánamo Bay, we tortured prisoners on the command of higher officers. We follow internal voting regulations that discriminate against whole classes of people. We allow animal research to be done every day that violates federal guidelines and never report the labs. We watch police brutality and never demand public review.

How else do we explain that slavery went on as long as it did, that domestic violence was called "their private business," that children showed up in school beaten and abused, and that sexual slavery—trafficking—continues to this day? Indeed, the list is embarrassingly long.

Obedience, the records show, is a very dangerous thing.

And yet, the role of obedience, of compliance with authority figures, in spiritual growth and development is obvious. It brings us to realize the value of learning to learn from others. And that in itself is both a duty and a revelation. By forgoing our own omnipotence, we leave ourselves room to gain from the experience of others.

But there is more than learning and guidance involved in obedience. Obedience has something to do with coming to terms with the self as well as with the status and experience of others. Bowing to the ideas, rank, and directions of those around us, we discover that it is really all right not to know everything. We come to see that the will of God for us is also manifested to us through others.

For years I had wanted to be a high school English teacher. I loved the power of fiction and drama to bring souls to feel feelings they might never know otherwise.

But by the time I got to the new school, they didn't need English teachers anymore and I found myself teaching my minor—history—instead. It took years to realize that, though I did not teach what I most wanted to teach that year, I did teach what I myself would most need in years to come—a review of both Church and world history. It was the will of God for me in disguise.

Accepting the guidance of others also brings us to a moment when we can let go, let others lead for a change, let ourselves do things in new ways and, ironically, also become new ourselves as a result. We can rest in the arms of God while the world goes on without having to depend on us. Our sole responsibility now is to begin to grow again.

By allowing others to take the tillers of our lives, to direct the development of our world, we give ourselves the opportunity to concentrate on other things. We let go of the soul's great need for achievement and choose for reflection instead. We become the thinkers rather than the doers of society for a change. It is a refreshing and liberating period in life. This willingness to allow the world to go its way without either our help or our interference gives the soul permission to breathe the fresh air of new ways of being alive.

At the same time, by resisting the challenges and leadership of others, we may be deliberately limiting not only our spiritual potential but our right to experiment with other ways of thinking. These very periods of life prepare us best for the phases of life yet to come. They are times to rethink the future, times to cultivate the "beginner's mind." They give us the opportunity to consider starting over. A period of new beginnings brings us into stark new awareness of the God who is infinite, who is creative, and who has more of life in mind for us.

In the end, then, freedom comes, first, from not having to be right and, second, from being willing to rethink our own principles and values and place in life. It is only then that we have the freedom to choose not only what we are willing to obey but why we are obeying it as well. Why we would or would not work for the fracking industry, for instance. Why we would or would not avoid a future in business, perhaps.

Then, the kind of moral reflection and dissent with which

the Milgram study confronts us becomes possible. We begin to discover that obedience becomes holy only when we know what we're doing and why we're doing it. Because a superior told me to, because the money is better, because other people expect me to, is simply not a good enough reason to take a path to a dead end, physically or morally. It is a less than fully human act to follow an order—a legal or social one—when it violates a moral or spiritual one.

The will of God is the only law worth keeping, the only law we are really required to keep. Obedience demands that we become as able to dissent as we are to obey. Any law that results in harm to another is a law to be suspected. Any law that violates the will of God for the good of the world is a law to be questioned. Any law that puts my submission to a system over the law of God is a law to be resisted.

The third step of humility, then, to submit "in all obedience" to anyone or anything, lies at the cutting edge of the soul. Very little that degrades an entire population or is intended to hurt any given group of people can possibly be moral. But it is the very responsibility to make that distinction that this step of humility is meant to protect.

Obedience is not for its own sake; it is for the preservation of the law of God. The Scriptures are clear about those differences. It is about learning to trust the moral compass of our own souls as well as to trust the authority, the insights of another. In the end it is humility, our total commitment to the glory and will of God—not obedience to the minions of any system, not to obedience for its own sake—that keeps us anchored to the mind of God. It is our commitment to the law of God that is our only true indicator and measure of the kind of attention we give to any system on earth.

The demon of unholy submission leaves us prey to pressures within us and around us that struggle for control. A spiritual life without an understanding that obedience is meant to free us to do the will of God is an incomplete and immature one.

A spiritual life that learns to listen to the voice of God within is a spiritual life with God as a director. Then we are free; then we are truly authentic.

*The Fourth Step of Humility*

# ENDURE THE PAINS
# OF DEVELOPMENT AND
# DO NOT GIVE UP

The fourth step of humility is "that [if] this obedience [is] under difficult, unfavorable, or even unjust conditions" we not grow weary or give up.

## *What is the challenge here?*

Some things in life cannot be avoided. Obedience, the sense of being beholden to someone else, is one of them. These issues start young—with parents and babysitters; with teachers; and with older siblings. Every new relationship along the way, at whatever age, is an exercise in control, theirs over us. To slip out of the noose of subordination, we work at learning to manipulate people by saying what they want to hear from us, for instance; by buying them off with favors or good work. Or we pout and have temper tantrums until we learn that those things don't really work. At best, they simply prolong the contest until we succumb, eventually, to an uneasy kind of peace that human conflict too often requires of children, of underlings, of subordinates.

The truth is that there is no real independence to be had in life. We are all attached forever to people who have claims on us—wives and husbands, employers and supervisors, social systems and government regulations, someone somewhere.

Accepting responsibility for our little part of life, however, doing the deed daily for years, with little interest, minimal support or personal excitement is its own kind of spiritual burden. Going on when there is nothing in the project interesting enough to engage me is not as noble as conscientious disobedience. But it can be twice as agonizing. Accepting directions that come down from some misty height, to do what I do not really enjoy doing, grates on the soul.

What to do then?

At that point, the combat shifts from control to endurance. Now, it's all about not growing weary—and oh, I have been weary enough so many times to understand the difficulty of going on. Then it's not that authority is oppressive or unfair. It's that the circumstances never change. The tiny little irritations that go with the situation never end. They become the sandpaper on my soul. I find myself in a No Exit moment: This is not going to change. It is never going to end.

I know that feeling only too well. My first teaching assignment at the age of nineteen, after one full year of college, was one hundred miles away from home. It was an era when nuns did not have cars or phones or even daily mail. Instead, intercommunity mail was sent in old envelopes marked "Kindness of" the person who was making the trip. If anyone ever did.

The weeks went slowly by. It was a long wait between periods of human interaction punctuated only by the grind of days in an elementary school classroom that never changed. The rounds of prayers, meals, college work, classroom preparation, and housecleaning went endlessly, monotonously on. All my peers had been sent to other places. Everyone else in the small convent was older, self-contained, intent on their own work, almost totally unaware of me or my very isolated social situation. There was nothing in the way of excitement. Actually, there was nothing but routine, dull and deadening routine. I prayed desperately to be moved. To ask to be moved would clearly have signaled the worst possible credentials for entering the community.

In addition to the schedule of the place, the local superior's speech pattern was gruff, not harsh necessarily, but not amenable to weakness either. It was time to think again about the fourth step of humility. What, I asked myself over and over, could possibly be the point of simply hanging on when most of all you want to quit? And what value is there, if any, to staying with something that leaves a person dry and bare inside? The great spiritual questions of my year were upon me, and I had no clue what the answer to either of those questions could possibly be.

I was too busy trying to save my mind as well as my soul.

When the next year's appointments were published in August, my heart sank. I was not moved to another mission; in the end I was sent back to the same place for the next three years. There was no avoiding it. I had to think through this step of humility and find not simply purpose but good in it. To be candid, it was years before I could see in retrospect what had really been happening to me when all I could do was hang on—and hope.

My first response to what I considered the most disappointing environment of my assignment became the unknown blessing of the time. The first of the next three years, I set about reading all the plays of Shakespeare. The second and third years, I read all the librettos of American musicals. Only years later did I realize that without what I considered that dull and dreary time, I would certainly not have been able to complete that library for years and years and years. The next assignment, when it finally came, captured every dimension of my soul. Life, then, was far too rich and stimulating for me even to begin to think of crawling into a room by myself to read something I did not need to read for any professional reason.

I forgot all about the grind of simply going on. Life had been resurrected—a kind of Mannheim Steamroller experience of the old made new again. All the pain of the past, I was sure was gone forever.

It took years before simply being able to endure became a factor again in my spiritual life. I did not at that time really see any basic or general or lifelong value in simply treading water anywhere. Better to be honest, I had by then come to believe. Better to be honest and quit. But I was wrong.

Actually, I came to realize then, it was better to find something else to do in the middle of the grind. Something that I really liked—like the reading regimen that had rescued my soul before. And so I did. That way, not only did the time go by fruitfully but I also began to enjoy my life more. I settled in. I quieted down. I lived a steady and deepening life. I discovered that simply being where I was, concentrating on the inner life rather than racing around looking for a more attractive exterior life, was itself a contemplative exercise.

I began to see that there was more value to simply being than first met the eye. I learned to make bad time good time, an enterprise that has made the entire rest of my life richer. I don't tap my feet in waiting rooms anymore. In the first place, I have something with me worth doing at all times. In the second, I know that there is no such thing as wasted time, unless, of course, I waste it. And finally, I have discovered in whole new ways that God's will is indeed best for me.

Little did I know then that endurance is itself a bulwark against the empty pride that comes with the delusion of autonomy. Little did I think back to what I had thought logical about the second step of humility: If God is really the Great Good of life, then the will of God is also best for us. And what is the will of God? Easy. God's will for us is what's left over when we have done everything we can possibly do to get out of doing what we're doing right now.

I learned that God's will was worth enduring—until the purpose of it could become transparent again and its gifts expose themselves. I learned that this is exactly what the fourth degree of humility is all about: learning, growing, living through the transition parts of life, and so becoming freer all the time.

## What is the underlying issue?

"O snail, climb Mount Fuji, But slowly, slowly . . ." the haiku master and lay Buddhist priest Issa writes. Some might call that a Japanese version of the fourth step of humility. Psychiatry might call it a recognition of the place of patience in life. The monastic might see it as a call to the virtue of endurance. But if endurance is such a universal part of life, what is the human question that drives it?

The haiku, in its short, sharp way makes three points:

In the first place, there are great, important things to do in life however small, however frail we feel, however stacked the odds are against us.

And yet, at the same time, there is more to life than speed. What's the use of speed? The mountain is not going to go anywhere as we climb it. Conditions might well change as we go and demand a revision of both our plans and our schedule.

Finally, of course, the difficulties involved in the project must be confronted head-on, but it's unlikely that they can be resolved immediately. After all, a mountain is a mountain with everything that has to say about what can be learned as we climb and everything that will need to be endured as we go.

Obviously, what is needed for the long haul is not heedlessness or a series of senseless attempts as we get more and more tired, more and more frustrated, more and more stressed. What is needed is patience.

It takes patience to come to know God. We must give ourselves a lifetime to do it.

It takes patience to appreciate every stage of the climb—the hard beginning, the lofty but unreal schedule, and, most of all, the wearying repetition of the process. We must be willing to immerse ourselves in each of them.

It takes patience to overcome the impulse to frustration,

the kind that comes from demanding from ourselves instantaneous results. Frustration ruins the journey by pushing on blindly, past the joy of the goals met and the sense of achievement in the understandings gained, and the comfort of security that comes from forming friendships along the way, and the joy of reaching one plateau after another. By allowing frustration to cloud our vision, we miss the scenes and views, the flora and fauna on the way.

This snail's journey is clearly, like the fourth step of humility, a call to live life with a quiet mind. Then, like the psalmist, we can "wait in patience for God's promise is forever" to help us do what must be done in us. This climb toward humility points us to the effect of frustration on the spiritual life and the spirit of patience it will take to succeed.

Frustration is what seeks to put us back in charge of our lives. It is the direct antithesis of humility. It stamps the foot of the soul and demands to be in control again. As a result, I abdicate the opportunity to learn something new either about myself or about life in general along the way. "I give up and grow weary" instead. I give up and grow angry or depressed instead. Just when I might have wrestled my egoism to the ground, I simply stop trying. The process is abandoned. My own growth is abandoned. I have put impatience with the will and ways of God where spiritual maturity should be.

Even more basic to self-understanding when these moods wash over me is the fact that it's not really any one particular thing that is my problem. What frustrates me is anything that obstructs my intent to wrench the world to my will. Down deep, frustration is not about the project at hand. It's my will that this is all about. It's about my internal insistence that my will be satisfied at all costs and immediately. Then I become a whimpering, silly kind of thing where only the strong can possibly prevail.

But there is a second question that demands at least as much reflection as the first, and perhaps even more depth. And that is the question of whether or not being patient in the face of injustice is not apathy. Why would anyone, let alone Benedict of Nursia, one of the greatest masters of spirituality in the history of the Church, advise endurance? Why call for patience even if this obedience is "under difficult, unfavorable, or even unjust conditions"? The answer demands serious consideration. What is the place of endurance in situations of abuse like bad marriages, demeaning professional environments, institutional oppression, and systemic injustice?

There are three major obstacles, I think, that must be confronted if we are to come to both physical and spiritual health in the face of spiritual and physical stress.

First, what is, is. To continue to pour salt on our own souls in the face of the natural impediments of life is to open ourselves to physical as well as spiritual discontent. Even chronic illnesses. What we continue to tell ourselves as we go—the self-talk that provides the script for our lives—determines our attitudes toward life in general. It dins into us that life is endemically unfair, perhaps. Or impossible, maybe. Or determined to defeat us, for all we know. It eats at the bedrock of faith. It distances us from the God within. It fails the test of trust in God. And, ironically, it makes the next challenge, the next project, the next long-term obstacle on the way to the will of God even harder to reshape because we have defeated ourselves even before we started.

Interestingly enough, what is now called the Stanford Marshmallow Study exposes the effect of patience in the present and its impact on the future as well. Working with children four to five years old, children too young to come to the situation with preconceived ideas, the researchers struck a deal. Each child was given a marshmallow. She or he could decide to eat it now or to wait fifteen minutes and get a second marshmallow for not having eaten the first.

Then the participants were followed throughout life to determine how they managed the twists and turns, the normal frustrations and failures of the average life. In each case, the years of scientific follow-up showed, those children who had delayed instantaneous gratification for the sake of long-term rewards in the initial experiment fared better on every scale of life development and achievement.

Clearly, patient endurance eases the kind of stress that modern medical science says actually kills people.

Second, there are simply some things in life that are not amenable to change or are totally outside our control to change. Disability, for instance. Imprisonment, for instance. Death, for instance.

It is only patient endurance in the face of such non-negotiables that enables us to withstand pressure with good mental health, let alone spiritual faith.

Patience and faith lead us on after moments like these still trusting in the future, still committed to living life to its psychological fullest, despite its physical boundaries.

Finally, there are things like slavery and war, sexism and racism, poverty and disgrace that can only be chipped away one generation, one life at a time. But to do that well, we must learn to endure. We must see the injustice, the difficulties before us, the unfavorable conditions in which we live and then work for years, if necessary, to make the future safe for others. That sense of purpose alone makes life rich and worthwhile, successful and significant, however limited the gains, however long the journey.

Generations of women have lived in oppression, raising children against all odds and working tirelessly, sometimes underground, for equality and justice. Generations of men have worked at jobs that broke them physically in order to provide for families they were left with few hours to enjoy and too little money to enable them to relax. Ever. Only after the formation of unions and the things like the Fair Labor Standards Act could men feel the fullness of dignity that comes with good, hard work well done. The African Americans who led the antislavery movements did not live in vain. Nor did they give up or succumb to the pressures around them. The Peace Movement inches closer every day to bringing the world to understand that pacifism is not passiveness. All of them climbing Mount Fuji slowly persist in making change one inch at a time.

Indeed, Scripture tells us clearly: God's time is not our time. We know neither the day nor the hour. It is ours only to go on working for change when going on seems fruitless and madness runs amok that is the true sign of both faith and commitment.

The point is that patient endurance climbs on, putting our lives in God's hands. We do consistently and faithfully what must be done to make this world a better place. No, we may not get the credit for doing it, and that in itself drains our efforts of the corrosive of pride. We trust only that our creating God will gather all the small pieces of effort and someday bring them together in a great new view of the world. Then we discover the power of patience.

Most of all, we are freed now from the infantilism of frustration. We are free to pursue the good—however long it takes to come. After all, it is the good we are about, not personal gratification. It is serenity, not security, that is the gift of patience.

The ancients explain it this way:

"How many snowflakes does it take to break a branch?" the snowy owl asked a snowflake.

"I don't know for sure, but it must be about a million," the snowflake answered back.

"And how many have fallen now?" the owl went on.

"Oh, I suppose about five thousand maybe," the snowflake calculated.

"Then why do you go on with such a fruitless task?" the snowy owl persisted.

"Because," the snowflake answered with a touch of exasperation, "I want to do my part."

*What are the spiritual implications of this step of humility?*

The place of patience in life is an important one. To confuse patience with compliance makes us all co-conspirators with all the evil in the world. On the other hand, to preach patience when what we really want is the right to be apathetic is about as far as we can get from the sharp, clear light of reason.

Nevertheless, the temptation to avoid shining the light of

truth into the dark spots of life abounds. "These things take time," people say when what they really mean is "I don't want to do anything to change it." Or "We have to be careful not to rock the boat," when what they really want is to avoid the consequences of conscience.

But Jesus makes plain the price of truth: "I have not come to bring peace but a sword," he says. There are times when conflict is the only cure for diseases of the soul. Societies mired in discrimination and legal exclusions stand blind to their own moral blindness. They begin to take as moral what are simply injustices masking as legal. They accept legalities, the purpose of which is to mask the dereliction they harbor. In those cases, there is no choice but to expose the sins such shadow boxes are designed to protect. It is not these things we are meant to endure.

Instead, endurance is the daily face of faith. It believes beyond all reasonable reason to believe that goodness can prevail, that the will of God will come when enough of us accept it, too. It is the living demonstration of belief in the God who created us to become the fullness of ourselves.

At the same time, endurance is not something that feels good. On the contrary. It is often dull and thankless. It's like training for a marathon. There's so much effort and, too often, so few results. It is the exercise regimen of the heart, the measure of the soul.

Exercise, the dull wearying repetition of stretch and squat and bar lift, has all the glamour of walking across the Sahara alone. It is torture in slow motion. And yet, without endurance, without the willingness to keep on keeping on, nothing the world ever needed would have happened.

The problem is that what is endured and won in one century must so often be won again in another. Just as the world thinks one struggle has been won, somewhere, somehow, it emerges all over again. We must be eternally vigilant about slavery, for instance, which is now sex slavery as well as economic slavery, and this new threat is one of global and horrendous dimensions. We must never assume that equality has been accomplished as long as the pursuit of power exists. Disease is never conquered without years of gainless research. Nor will justice come without daily efforts. Injustice must be addressed but may well not be achieved for eons, in which case our mantra must become "If not for us, then because of us."

Endurance, the unsung champion of the spiritual life, has a great deal more to offer me than social honor or civic support. On the spiritual level, it is self-absorption, the universal I, the egotistic center of the cosmos, against which we struggle day after day.

And yet, in all these circumstances, both personal and public, it is the awareness of the power of patience and the energy that comes with endurance that make a difference in both the substance and the quality of our lives.

Most important of all, perhaps, is the realization that endurance and acceptance are not the same thing. It is one thing to work through difficult questions and tangled relationships one small step at a time. It is another thing entirely to accept the abuse or the denigration that may go with them. To understand that changes in male-female status may take years, sometimes even generations, to grow into is only realistic. These ideas are bred into a culture and are difficult, even painful, to uproot. But to argue in the face of clear concepts to the contrary that such changes are unnecessary or useless to strive for is immoral.

To continue to bar young girls entrance into school, for instance, because there are no toilet facilities on the property—as is common around the world—is totally unacceptable. If school systems cannot or do not provide facilities, international development groups must insist on building them.

A recourse to principles, a commitment to the will of God for the entire world, is in order. Whenever harm is done to the full development of other human beings—when bodily harm, as in female genital mutilation, is defended as a religious act or a cultural custom—debate is no longer an option. Time is of the essence now, discussion is unacceptable. Why? Because the intellectual future of the next generation, of half the population, is in jeopardy. We may need to endure long and tedious negotiation to repair these issues, but we cannot even begin to think of accepting such things as cultural norms.

No doubt about it, endurance is the cement of human development, one of the few warranties we have these days of possible salvation of the human race. The ability to say no to myself, to the oppression of others, is the one assurance we have that human beings are teachable, are capable of becoming fully human, can change, can be saved from themselves. Because we have the patience to bear hard things, we can work through the nuclearization of the world, we can transcend racism, we can become a united planet of chain-linked nations, we can become a society of equals.

By learning to bear hard things well, we secure the future of the human race as well as our own ability to survive. By being willing to put our personal power down in favor of someone else's vision and experience, we pledge ourselves to benefit from the power and goodness of others. We save ourselves from our own limitations and follies, from our lack of maturity and experience. Most of all, we pledge ourselves to be open to the wisdom figures of life and so become wiser ourselves as we go.

Without endurance we succumb silently to the demons of injustice. We dry up inside, shrivel in our hope, and belie the will of God for the world.

On the other hand, a spirituality of endurance frees us from the rampages of destructive pride. It opens us to a community of wisdom figures, guides who, if we will only allow it, are there to lead us through the ravages of our time.

*The Fifth Step of Humility*

# ACKNOWLEDGE FAULTS AND STRIP AWAY THE MASKS

The fifth step of humility is that "we do not conceal from the abbot or prioress any sinful thoughts entering our hearts . . . but rather confess them humbly."

## *What is the challenge here?*

After coming to grips with the kind of God we believe in and committing ourselves to living in harmony at every level of life with what that creating God wills for creation, we begin to move beyond even the spiritual narcissism that marks an incessant preoccupation with being spiritual. In the third and fourth steps of humility we open ourselves to the wisdom figures around us and commit ourselves to not running away from the growth moments in life.

Now this fifth step of humility brings us to the great encounter with the self. It's perhaps one of the most demanding moments of all. It confronts us with our selfishness, yes, but also with our own standards of perfection.

After all, it's not possible to reveal our sinful self—to face the demons that have mastered us—until we decide what sin really is and which sins have us in captivity now. At this moment.

The question now is, On what standard of perfection do we operate? In what do we strive to be perfect?

One of the more shocking elements of monastic life for me in the 1950s and '60s was a practice called the "manifestation of faults." That custom had begun as a kind of spiritual direction program between seekers and the monastics of the desert centuries before. By the mid-twentieth century, at least where I was, it had clearly deteriorated into nothing more than a recitation of personal failings in monastic life. The entire community gathered in the refectory after supper every Friday night while one part of the group or another would "speak fault." It was a highly formal event. Every sister had been given a list of common "faults"—spilling food and water, wasting soap and electricity, breaking silence, walking fast—which she was required to recite. If she had received a personal correction during the week, for instance, for "laughing loudly at recreation," she added that as well, and ended by begging the superior for a "penance."

Every week it was the same: The Chapter of Faults opened with a prayer and a reading from the gospels. After each sister "confessed" and asked for a "penance," the community said a psalm together and the process was over for another week.

Frankly, nothing of any moment ever happened there. The entire event was sheer formula. It was, in fact, an irritation for

sisters and superiors alike, an uncomfortable and basically useless event. Many sisters, in fact, brought books to read while
a line of other sisters droned through the list of peccadilloes.
Everyone there knew that the things to be said were without
moral substance. Nor were they erasable from the catalog of
human behaviors, even if anyone had seriously set out to do so.

It was a community custom salvaged from the spirituality
of the early monastic communities and, I was sure, meant to
fulfill the call to transparency implied in this fifth step of humility. But by now it had simply become part of the schedule,
a piece of the furniture of religious life. No one there ever said
anything we all didn't know and weren't "reciting" ourselves.
No one, I'm sure, was ever saved by the process, but some
might certainly have been plagued by it, if for no other reason
than its utter emptiness. Its meaninglessness.

The Chapter of Faults was, at very most, nothing more
than a symbolic admission of human sinfulness. It was hardly
any kind of genuine confession. "Spilling water, losing pins,
and spotting scapulars" never rose to the level of morality or
reflected the gentle depth of spiritual direction either.

Instead, this formalized process had only come to confuse
the entire issue of what it was in the human heart that actually
obstructed a person's relationship with God. Was the chapter
about the foibles of human nature? The matter being recited
was certainly not conscience matter. If anything, it blurred the
lines between the moral, the immoral, and the amoral. What
were we doing and why were we doing it? I wondered. Was
this nothing more than a ritual of control and submission?

And yet it was from these fragments of the past, like shards
of pottery discovered in an ancient archaeological dig, that I

came to understand what it was that was missing in my own life. And even in the lives of the people around me. People everywhere, in all walks of life, I began to see, were just as trapped as I was. Only differently. Women labored under the rubric of what it meant to be a "good woman," a supermom. Good women baked cookies. Really good mothers did not get jobs outside the home. Good fathers worked hard, harder, hardest to get less and less out of life. And worried more and more as the years went by about not having been a "good father." It was a world full of shoulds and musts and social standards parading as theology.

We all had standards of perfection developed out of social norms and made to seem moral. We all substituted a set of false norms and called it perfection.

As the years went by, as a prioress myself concerned for the spiritual development of seekers in the twenty-first century, I began to recognize what this ancient wisdom literature, the Rule of Benedict, was signaling us to remember. The message was achingly clear: Everyone carries a burden too heavy to ignore. Each of us has something to confront, something that is scarring our soul, something for which we have yet to be forgiven, or have not yet grappled with, even by ourselves. Each of us needs someone else to help us with it. Only one thing was clear: A practice like this was not the help that was needed, perhaps, but the reality was surely worth struggling with.

There is in each of us a gaping hiatus of the soul, a rupture of the wholeness which we seek. This is the silent secret with which we struggle all our lives. It takes the shape of an unresolved relationship, perhaps, a broken piece of our integrity, maybe, a wound for which there is no balm, a compulsion that holds us captive and limits our growth.

Somewhere we have experienced something which we have not shared, a burden of soul we have yet to confront. There is something burrowed within us that is stopping us from being the fullness of ourselves. There is something we regret that we cannot yet unburden because no one now understands what happened in that time so far away. There is no one, not one, left from there to forgive us or free us or strengthen our faith in the place of struggle in our life. The time, the distance, the deaths between then and now have covered over what needs to be uncovered if I am ever to be new again.

For me, it was a home life forged in conflict, in religious differences, in addictions too binding to share, too foreign to trust to a group like my sisters in the Chapter of Faults. No one here would even be able to imagine the kinds of stories I would tell.

We can paper such things over with work and pray they will go away. Yet, all the while, these past realities have something to do with every day and decision of our present lives.

The struggle within us has left a scar. This memory that we hide in the cave of our heart does not go away. Instead, it leaves us full of pain, aching for wholeness. No number of masks and confession games heals it.

It is an emotional catharsis, a spiritual insight, that is needed here, not a legal or ecclesiastical one. An emotional catharsis comes from following the pain to its source, by admitting the breach of soul, and by being willing to reframe its effects. It comes from facing the hurt that is eating away at the heart. It is abated by acknowledging the rupture I have caused or nursed or repressed or left to turn to cement in my soul. It demands then that I commit myself to making life new again. It is not about spilling food and water.

It is a great moment.

Since those early days in religious life, I have known many new beginnings. All of them were personal. All of them were real—meaning they had an impact on me as a person. All of them required that I begin again to figure out what life was about, what I was meant to be about, where I was on the path. And each of them led me to more freedom, more depth.

Changes at every level of life are commonplace to me now. I have been able to survive so many of them. So, I know enough not to expect to be able to stem them. They are out of my control or beyond my present understanding. But they are not without gift. They become the seedbed of the soul, these regular skirmishes with life. Eventually, I came to know, old struggles fade and life rights itself again, a testimony to sorrow and confession. Or the experience of strong contrary opinions keeps the self at the task of rethinking life, of staying open to its possibilities, of being willing to go on imagining new ways of being alive.

Whatever the evolution of life, old struggles morphed into new possibility. And I grew, however slowly.

Point: Sin, brokenness, as the Church has always said, can be a "happy fault," an invitation to a new beginning. It calls us to reflect on the way we live and think and direct our lives until we can change our bearings once again. It is this unending grace of change that is the tether to which we cling as the waves of life shred the sails that have brought us to this point.

But silent admission is not enough. For that, the steps of humility have a clearer message. Growth is a process, an unending process, they teach us: Reflect on the pain. Discern its origin. Find models whose own experiences can help to reconstruct its meaning. And, most of all, understand that confession—the unburdening of the past—is never too late. On the contrary, confrontation of the unfinished parts of ourselves and self-revelation is forever the key to freedom from the past as well as freedom for the future.

## *What is the underlying issue?*

It is one thing to talk, as the Rule does, about self-revelation as a step to humility. After all, who would doubt that? What's left of hubris, of image, of pretense once we begin to expose the secrets of the soul? But, we have a right to wonder if superiors won't use the information against us. If friends won't reject us. If even the wisdom figures among us might not turn away from us. Those are fair concerns and deserve a great deal of thought before we begin to talk to anyone whose own spiritual depths are uncertain or whose ability to keep a confidence is in question.

And yet, the far more important question in a day of private communications that are now forever public is, What happens to the person who does not deal with the secrets of the heart? What kind of energy can a person bring to life who allows the past to clog the arteries of the mind? How confident can a person be who lives with the stress of exposure? How emotionally stable is a person who spends life ignoring the Achilles' heel that could well spill over into embarrassment—or even break down—at any time? And finally, how capable of helping others are those who harbor their own need to hide from themselves?

At the end of the day, on the edge of public rejection, only humility can save us from the terror of exposure. After all, once having exposed ourselves, we can never be hurt again by the risk of ruthless revelation.

Psychologists are confirmed in their opinion that what we spend our lives trying to keep secret is what stands to poison us most. It's not so much what other people say about us that endangers us. It's what we cannot admit about ourselves—even to ourselves—that most threatens to undermine our confidence, our competence, and even our sense of self-esteem. If we ourselves are not sufficient to ourselves, if we struggle with a sense that something is missing in us, who else can we expect to possibly find us worthy?

The research is clear: Secrets affect the secret keeper's quality of life. They take the spirit that should be expended on both giving and getting the best out of life and turn it inward.

Secret keepers become preoccupied with themselves: with their fear of public nakedness and their efforts to make sure that the secret never oozes out accidentally. When conventional wisdom insisted, for instance, that adopted children should never discover that they were adopted, let alone the identities of their birth mothers, more energy was spent on hiding than on living. Families lived in mortal combat with the hidden enemy: truth.

I, on the other hand, had been brought up knowing my real

name, knowing that there were two sets of lives in my living, understanding that identity was a very slippery thing. And as a result, having no secret to hide, no shame to conceal. What could have been a barrier became freedom from fear for me.

With the fear of public unmasking comes low self-esteem, a homegrown, built-in mistrust of myself. The impulse to brick myself in, safe from the rest of the world while my world gets smaller and smaller, is by my own design. I have become a prisoner of myself.

The issues we're afraid to share, the things that rankle in the soul but never get seriously examined, the researchers tell us, trigger an even greater search for meaning. We become rudderless, without compass, stuck in our aloneness with nowhere clear to go. The secret that lies within has control now.

And through it all, the fifth step of humility invites us to accept the antidote to our fear—self-revelation with someone who can treat our scars caringly and lovingly. Then, the liberation inherent in the fifth step of humility is plain. We are freed from our self-hatred, from the bonds of deceit, from the desire to hide ourselves where the world can never see us.

And all of this in a time when the internet, its blogs, its oversharing, and its new outreach denude us for all the world to see. Seduced by anonymity, looking for the private revelation we need to untangle our complicated selves, we say things on a heartless, uncaring social medium which, ironically, will never, ever be really private again. We, who have spent life refusing to tell a single person where it hurts, tell the whole world now. And at once. Hidden still, but looking for community to heal the wounds we are carrying alone.

And so the fear of exposure becomes, in this internet age, a paradox of privacy in public form. But with no guarantee of either loving care or professional expertise for the effort.

Benedict of Nursia has been called the Great Psychologist by those who study his Rule and marvel at his understanding of human development. In this step of humility, he is particularly astute. His concern is not for sinfulness in the negative sense of the word but for the effects of sin and brokenness in all our lives. It is surely also a sin when we refuse to deal with the emotional detritus that weighs us down. Without addressing our brokenness, whatever burdens we carry—either as natural parts of life or by our own hands—stand to block our growth.

Clearly, Benedict in this sixth-century Rule wanted members to honor their need for companions in this journey of self-worth and self-respect and self-sufficiency. He talks about wrestling with the muddled, raveling self with a loving companion. In this case, it is the abbot or the prioress who is mandated by the same Rule to see themselves as the Good Shepherd intent on saving the isolated, the abandoned, the straying sheep. But the basic point is clear: We all need someone who will hold our lives in loving hands as we grow.

Benedict's fifth step of humility is meant to be a model of love, of development, of care, and of growth. And, in the end, this step liberates us from false expectations and useless posturing, which destroy us even as they pose as salvific.

No doubt about it: Such self-revelation was always meant to be about more than spilling food and water.

*What are the spiritual implications of this step of humility?*

What can be more frightening than the thought of having to face headlines that rip open my private life, leaving me unveiled and vulnerable to all the forces of nature around me? Now the church knows . . . Now my friends know . . . Now my colleagues know . . . Now my family knows. Except what if there is nothing disparaging to find out about me? Then what harm can anyone do to me?

The social and spiritual ramifications of the open life are totally disarming. Once I say "I am an alcoholic," what else can anyone say to embarrass me about that? When I finally admit, "My father died in prison," what will they use against me? When I confess that in a fit of postpartum depression I tried to smother my last child, who will accuse me of what now? After they find out that I was indicted for embezzlement, what can they intimidate me with? What can they do when they discover that I'm gay if I've already told people that myself?

I have sat in offices for years and watched frightened people draw new breath once the worst was said and nothing bad happened as a result.

Better yet, perhaps, what can obstruct my own growth and potential once I'm no longer hiding from the world? I have now separated myself from the false image that has grown up around me. Having trusted someone to walk with me through my worst fears, I can afford to trust the whole world again. I have found wisdom and understanding enough in someone else to enable me to finally even trust myself.

There is no substitute for such a moment of spiritual rebirth, of psychosocial health, of public fearlessness. What can anyone else do to me now? What can they tell about me that I have not told about myself? It is a moment of new growth, of renewed promise. The world is mine to embrace again.

The truth is that self-revelation is the one thing that can end the game of charades I've been playing. I am now released from anyone's and everyone's false expectations. I can just be myself and that will be enough. In fact, it will have to be enough because there is nothing left to be secret about anymore. The talking can stop. All the wondering can cease now. The truth has been told and the world has not ended as a result. Ah, sweet relief.

Even more astounding is the fact that I am finally rescued from the burden of perfection because the world knows now that I'm not. No one needs to measure me by any measurement other than the obvious. Yes, I'm a gambler. Yes, I never graduated from college. Yes, I had an abortion. And I grew stronger, greater, and more compassionate with other people for that very reason. The rewards of exposure know no end.

"Those who swallow a stone become a stone," the adage says. And counselors tell us that the struggles we hide only serve to consume our energies and sour our psyches. It's time to put down the burden of silence, to live better and freer in the light than can ever be done in the dark places of life. It's time to be ourselves. To be truly who we say we are. To abjure the temptation to exaggerate our credentials or heighten our pedigree. To risk the possibility of rejection by people we shouldn't want to be approved by anyway.

Indeed, once we admit who we are, fearlessness takes over. We are suddenly invincible. Why? Because nothing can frighten us any more than what we felt when no one knew anything about us but whose very lack of information kept us in chains.

Life takes on a completely different hue once we tell just one person what it is that we've worked so hard at not saying. Yes, all our delusions of grandeur die. But in that case, we can't possibly be disappointed by what we cannot dream of having in life.

More than that, our self-righteousness dies, too. Not only are we capable of seeing ourselves and understanding ourselves and why we did what we did, but we can now understand others as well. I'm ready at long last to take my place among the healers and the truth tellers in society. I'm ready now to hold up others as others once supported me. These are the ones who, just like me, need to be freed from the "great masquerade" that is choking their souls. Like me, they have gone through life with no hope of finding someone they can trust. Now it is time for me to be there for them.

A woman in her seventies, worn down by the shame of it all, appeared at my door, emotionally exhausted and distraught. "I have to tell you something," she said. And then, though her story was garbled and disjointed, she poured it all out. She had been abused regularly as a child by her seminarian brother, the apple of her mother's eye, who she knew would never believe anything bad of him. There was no one who could help her, no one to turn to. She had been working with a psychiatrist for years, making very little progress, but had said nothing about this trauma to the doctor. Maybe because he was a man, maybe because he was a public figure. Now, though, having told one person, she was finally free of the fear of talking about it and the breakthrough came quickly. But, oh, far, far, too late.

Softened by having learned to accept myself, I have something honest to tell other people. Once I stop using the condemnatory language of the streets, those who see themselves as outcasts can hear the understanding they're looking for in my voice. It is a magnet for those who have heard nothing but condemnation—their own or everyone else's—all their lives. It is a tone made in heaven so that a bit of heaven can start here for everyone.

As Mary Lou Kownacki writes, "Who is it that we would not love, if we only knew their story?" And on the other hand, who can we truly love if we do not embrace our own story?

The demon of secrecy stunts our growth and clips our wings. Without the process of self-revelation and the genuine humility it brings, we doom ourselves to go on hiding within ourselves forever. We have chained ourselves to the eternal disguise of a false self that demands more and more trappings behind which to hide. We will never come to the liberating relief of the true self.

With the courage of self-revelation, on the other hand, the humility that comes frees us for the fullness of life. After all, the attempt to feel better about ourselves by collecting empty symbols of adulation and power, we know now, never really changes much at all. But one thing is finally clear: We don't need the lies and subterfuges and image making anymore. Now all we need is the awareness that to be myself is all the self I have and it is enough.

*The Sixth Step of Humility*

# BE CONTENT WITH
# LESS THAN THE BEST

The sixth step of humility is to be "content with the lowest and most menial treatment."

### *What is the challenge here?*

I read an article recently entitled "Ten Most Expensive Useless Things to Buy." Among them were a million-dollar box of chocolates, a $68,500 cricket ball, a $225,000 bottle of liquor, and a $130,000 TV. "What else is needed for total happiness?" the article asked.

It stopped me for a moment. This had to be a joke. But no, not only were these things available for sale but the bottle of liquor and the cricket ball had already been bought. It was the most expensive list of trinkets I had ever seen. What is it, I wondered, that could possibly prompt anyone to buy anything like this? And what does it have to do with the spiritual life? With the emotional life? With any kind of real life at all?

One thing for sure: The Twelve Steps of Humility—Benedict's distillation of Benedictine communal spirituality—recognize the allure and the danger of such an exaggerated, profligate attitude toward life.

Yet, if any of the steps are designed to refresh our thinking, to stretch us, this one is surely it.

In my own life, the sixth step of humility, with its call to constraint, has been a constant prod. But to what? The very wording of it stops my heart in midbeat and spins the world around. Stark and short, blunt and unforgiving, we are, it says, to be "content with the lowest and most menial treatment." I winced at that one in the early years. And I still wince a bit now. The American mind rebels: Lowest? Most menial? Impossible. Unacceptable. Approaching the ridiculous. After all, this is the twenty-first century.

Right. And, as if written especially for this moment and place in time, the sixth step of humility forced me to look again and again at the way I was living it. It required me even more to ask myself what my life was becoming as I went on. Was it simpler? Or more complex by the day? Worse, had I become indifferent to the whole issue?

When we were new members in the community, up until the mid-1960s, they gave each of us three habits, three coifs or headbands, three veils, and two pair of shoes. One set was for Sundays, one for daily wear, one for work. I figured then that there was nothing much to think about where the sixth step of humility was concerned. It had already been decided. But I feel very differently about that now. There is, in fact, a great deal more to think about here than counting blouses or having more than two pair of shoes. And all of it touches a person very deeply, very specifically.

Instead of simply expecting things from the system, like uniform clothes or institutional furniture, I found myself required to choose carefully now. Like everyone else, we were children of our age. Like Israelites climbing the Tower of Babel, we knew ourselves to be the generation for which the sky was indeed the limit.

I watched the years go by—as we shifted away from a universal desire for "enough" to a deep-down spiritual ache for everything in sight. To a sense of deprivation in affluence. But more than that, to the very inflation of the sense of self and the ballooning of grand expectations. I came to understand that the sixth step of humility was about more than consumerism and the amassing of goods. What is every bit as important as the amassing of things in Benedictine spirituality is the danger of getting seduced by delusions of grandeur. And that's where humility comes in.

One day something happened that made it all glaringly clear: I was in an island country as the guest of a friend. He'd just bought a native cottage on a small piece of land that fronted the sea. He'd added a tiny kitchen, a minimum of sewage and electricity, and, best of all, a large screened-in porch. Most of all, he was, as the Scripture said, "going out to the highways and byways and inviting people in"—no rent asked, no fees applied. Which is exactly how I got there. We slept on cots and couches and in one tiny bedroom. We lived on the big, broad porch and ate canned tuna and local fish. It was a magical place. After all, the breeze was soft, the sea clean and clear as an aquamarine, the rain was fierce and untamed and soul-searing. It was an excursion into the natural and the real and the enough. And more than that, it was a display of selfless generosity.

On Monday, I went the couple of miles to the small hotel down the single-lane road to check in with the office back home. There was a small, tense American woman beside me at the only bank of pay phones on the island. And she was very angry. Her voice was getting higher and higher, more and more angry. "I paid plenty to come down here," she said, "and this is a mess. You people told me that it was a beautiful sunny spot and all we've had for three days is rain, pouring down rain." I heard a few words from the even-sounding voice on the other end, but she broke in again. "I want out of here. Today." A few more words on the other end and then, "What do you mean there are no planes until Thursday! This is a disgrace. I will never use your agency again! And I have no intention of paying you!" Then she banged the phone down and tromped away.

If there were anything in modern life that cried our loud for the sixth step of humility, this had to be it!

Things in themselves, I understood, are far outside the confines of Benedict's sixth step. Rather than to wealth and power, this step is a universal call to become the kind of person who can tell the difference between self and nonself, between the true self and the false self, between having enough and demanding privilege. It is a call to go through life with a very finely measured notion of what it really is that makes for freedom and for authenticity. For authenticity, for sure.

All of which is fine to say years later, but in those first years of the spiritual search in a rapidly encompassing material world, the confusion such statements stirred up in my soul was genuine—and disconcerting. It was clear that Benedictine spirituality was light-years away from what my world taught me was even dignified, let alone successful. Or properly ambitious. Or the good life. Or progress. But what else was there? The answer was easier now: It was about being "content with the lowest and most menial treatment."

In this new world, everything of importance, it seems, is measured in things. Things that are bigger—meaning better, meaning modern. Like bigger cars or bigger computers or bigger wardrobes or bigger plans. As heirs of financial-technological societies, getting ahead is what we're about. To even suggest anything else seems so out of sync with the essence of what it means to be human now. Here in the West at least. And yet, what can we possibly do about it in what is, by nature, a culture of accumulation?

Most of all, what does that have to do with my personal level of spirituality? Just because I live in a country of cheap clothes and mass production centers?

At one level it is a serious conundrum. At another level, I realized one day when I reread "are content with the lowest and most menial treatment" that this small step toward humility could have been written expressly for this culture at this time. Or for any culture and for each of us who find ourselves slipping into the malignancy of commercial engorgement, of wanting the "more" of Madison Avenue life to the detriment of all life's other gifts. Because in a world of things by which to measure our human progress or declare our status, it is oh, so easy, so natural a thing to do.

I was arranging the relics of my life on the open shelves in my office one day—feeling a little guilty, if truth were known, that I even had such things. Each of the small pieces—a set of worry stones from China, a carved Bible stand from Africa, a candle from a Benedictine abbey in Europe—was a sign to me of the affection that has carried me through the dry spots in life. The pictures, the mementos, the little gifts that have a meaning no one but I can possibly know, touch an untouchable part of life. Were these my priceless trinkets, like the million-dollar box of chocolates and the $68,000 cricket ball they were selling on the internet these days?

Then I recited the sixth step of humility to myself again—to be "content with the lowest and most menial treatment . . ." And this time, I got it. This step of humility isn't really about whether we should have things or not, as important as that may be to the spirit of simplicity. The statement is clear: It's about the treatment we come to expect from the world around us that makes the difference between humility and narcissism, between simplicity of life and overbearing self-importance. It's about the American woman who expected the world to get her out of the rainstorm that inconvenienced her vacation. Today. And to return her ticket money as well.

The fundamental question the sixth step of humility raises, I finally realized, is not so much what I have but why I expect it and need it and demand it.

This step of humility, to be "content with the lowest and most menial treatment," is more about walking into a room and not expecting to sit in the best chair. It's not about whether I own the chair. It's about not assuming that I should never have to wait in line to talk to the bank manager like the rest of the population. It's about learning never to expect public attention, free tickets, and special mention. It's a matter of learning to go through life like the Jesus who was laid in a manger, lived as a carpenter, and died on a cross.

There is, it seems to me now, one issue that connects an obsession for things, an addiction to status, and the tendency to an exaggerated sense of self. It is the spiritual superficiality that comes from a fundamental confusion between the true self and the false self. The true self has no secrets from itself and harbors no notions of being the center of the universe, however large or small the universe at issue may be. The true self is happy with the self that it is.

My false self, on the other hand, is extremely unhappy and works to hide its fundamental smallness even from my own consciousness. To present an image of success and stature, I spend my life building and buying the camouflage that makes me look like more than I am and even what I'm not. I buy for the sake of display. I posture for the sake of special attention. I check the internet to see how important I am. I race from thing to thing, from place to place looking for the proper respect, the right amount of adulation. But in the end, it never comes. There is never enough of that kind of thing to satisfy an ego inflated on importance. Which means that, in the end, real freedom is bartered for the glitter of nothing because freedom is not about being important. Freedom is about not needing to be important.

At base, the sixth step of humility brings us to confront the struggle to understand the distinction between arrogance and authenticity. It's the search for authenticity, for the true self, the self without expectations, that frees us to be happy wherever we are. Because when we don't expect anything, we can't be disappointed.

The need to have more trinkets, the need to be noticed, the need to be thought to be more than I am entraps us. And that, I think, is when the sixth step of humility cries for attention.

It is the humility that comes from practicing this step that frees me from the glut of things, the obscenity of pretense, the expectation of special attention. Then I discover authenticity, the true me, for which no amount of social camouflage can ever substitute.

### What is the underlying issue?

There is nothing in the sixth step of humility and its call for simplicity, authenticity, and self-effacement that speaks of attractiveness to a modern world.

"Getting ahead," at least in a modern culture—if not in most of the high-end economies of the world—smacks of getting things, getting power, getting status, getting noticed. Of the four, the trend is definitely toward getting status and getting noticed. Being seen with the right people, going to the right places, getting the right parking spots, and being ushered to the head tables is premium.

But the sixth step of humility instructs us not to want any kind of special treatment at all, which implies, of course, that special treatment has nothing to do with genuine freedom. In a document far removed from the average personal advice column, we're told to be "content with the lowest and most menial treatment." So what are we to think? Where does happiness lie in a consumer society if not in consumption?

There are two great intellectual divides in the happiness discussion today. The first lies in the history of the struggle to define happiness. The second lies in the emerging science of happiness.

The first deals with the musings of philosophers, poets, and artists down the ages as they struggled with the role of pleasure, the ever-present specter of disaster despite all happiness to the contrary, and the meaning of life. Aristotle taught that happiness requires "being involved in virtuous activity." Doing something, in other words, that is good for humankind.

The second lies in the newly founded science of happiness. Happiness, social scientists say, is a matter of our natural disposition, the circumstances we're facing, and the way we normally deal with life. Some people are naturally positive under pressure, some circumstances are more demanding than others, some of us simply respond better or more effectively to life's natural difficulties.

Both theories of happiness are sound. Both are helpful. Both are good. But neither of them has anything to say about what happens when life's circumstances are outside our control. What happens to our happiness when the sky darkens and the path through a hard time is not clear? What happens when even the will to do something about making ourselves happy is absent? Then, the sixth step of humility has a great deal to say to a world that looks outside itself for happiness.

The Rule gives us three criteria by which to assess our likelihood of ever being truly happy. Not simply satisfied, that is, but genuinely contented with life. Happy.

First, if you have not attached your sense of self to having the best of everything, you won't be crushed when you see someone with things that cost more than yours. You'll be happy to simply have what you truly need to function. Like a decent car that can get you across town, maybe. Or a small yard to plant a few flowers, maybe. Or a good dog to keep you company in that small apartment and a good book to read.

Second, if you don't need to be the center of attention, you will be happy just to be part of a group of good people who do good things together. The thirst for attention is a toxic brew. If it comes—in athletics, in government, in public activities— you will be scrutinized to the point of depression. And if it doesn't, you'll be depressed, too.

Third, if you don't expect a constant deluge of privilege and preeminence, then not experiencing those things will not disturb you. You will be just as pleased with general admission tickets as you'd be in the box seats. After all, it's the same show.

The Rule is straightforward: If you do not depend on exemption, advantage, and personal prerogatives to measure your happiness, your success, your bliss in life, life will become its own reward. A walk by the lake at night will dilute all the pressures of the day. An appointment for supper with friends will be enough to get you up happy in the morning. Then whatever the turn of the social system around you, your love of life unadorned and unaffected will sustain you.

The Rule strikes at the heart of the kind of pride that can be healed by the kind of humility that makes the ego invulnerable. If we do not need the adulation or attention of others to give us a sense of self-worth, then to be treated as a commoner becomes an uncommonly significant and unconscious blessing.

The sixth step of humility gives us the opportunity to come to know ourselves in the raw. What we are without masks and costumes to protect us from the eyes of the world is where real happiness lies. Even more, humility allows others to know us stripped down to the bone. It is a moment of clarity. It tells us that we are enough for ourselves. It gives us the opportunity to become everything we are, everything we can be, rather than find ourselves pinioned on the false opinion of others.

Humility punctures all the definitions of happiness a world made of plastic and glass has to offer. Instead of glitter, it's about authenticity, simplicity, truth. It's about being exactly who we are, no more, no less. It's about being satisfied with enough rather than being intoxicated with the dregs of excess. It's about being open enough to be insulated from the breakdown of the false impressions we've spent a lifetime fabricating.

Humility spares us from having to put on airs, to keep up, to impress, or to mask. We don't need to pretend that we are anyone we aren't. We only need to become the best of what we are.

In retrospect, then, they are all correct about happiness. The philosophers, the social scientists, and this ancient spiritual document all take us beyond the superficial to the essentials of life. Happiness, they show us, is about more than things, more than prestige, more than somebody else's opinion of success. To know how to cultivate happiness ourselves rather than simply wait to get it prefabricated or prepackaged is the essence of what it means to be free, to be authentic, to be real.

Aristotle says that happiness is about living well and doing well. It's about avoiding excess and devoting myself to the highest dimensions of life—moral, spiritual, cultural, and social. It means living with a clear conscience. It means living a rich spiritual life. It means immersing myself in the best of the arts, the best of sports, the best of people. Because these are the things that make me a whole person, a person of good heart and clear mind who lives to benefit others as well as myself.

Martin Seligman, father of the Positive Psychology Movement, says that we are each born with a natural capacity for the positive in life. We're each born with a predisposition to optimism or pessimism, in other words, and we can learn to think our way out of the debilitating aspects of what we label the negative. We can shape our understanding and our desires and our attitudes in ways that are more life-giving than destructive, both of us and of our world.

Finally, the Rule of Benedict tells us what at least some of that shaping involves: We must be willing to accept who we are. We must avoid becoming seduced by the accoutrements of false identity. We must be willing to be "content with the lowest and most menial treatment." Then, we will never spend our lives waiting for more than that.

The sixth step of humility is the antidote to social rejection, to fear of public exposure, to jealousy, to false expectations. The sixth step of humility steeps us in authenticity and frees us to be enough for ourselves.


*What are the spiritual implications of this step of humility?*

I remember so well, too well perhaps, my invitation to speak at a very prestigious university. I had packed my own doctoral gown, for the occasion which is the custom for such academic events, and was carrying it. But in the car on the way to the lecture hall, they told me that they didn't allow any gown but their own to be used. I said, "Well, in that case, I won't wear a gown at all. I'll speak in my suit."

After all, I figured, if my gown wasn't good enough for their stage, why invite me in the first place? After all, it was the gown I earned at my own university that had gotten me there. And this was no time to begin to pretend that I was something I'm not.

It is precisely to the acceptance of the real in our lives—the authentic, the honest—that the sixth step of humility calls us.

The circumstances in which we find ourselves are the material out of which we must make our lives. To avoid what is, to want to be someone or something we are not, is the ultimate abandonment of the life in which we are meant to grow to full stature. Otherwise, when we look back at where we've been, what can we ever see except masquerade? Who and what will we ever know ourselves to be? When we ask ourselves what we have done with our lives, what will we list: the awards, the trophies, the money, the things we've bought, or the people we've cared for, the ideas we've promoted, the truth we've told? Will we ever be able to say, "I became myself by being myself and doing everything I could do for others"?

The key to choosing what is authentic in life and keeping our own integrity at the same time lies in tending always in the direction of simplicity. It is a cry to develop a sense of enoughness. To learn to be happy with enough money, enough attention, enough success, and enough comfort takes the senseless striving and accumulating and hoarding and competing out of life. It leaves us with more than status. It leaves us with a life worth living.

The problem is that modern culture itself encourages us to play at who we are long before we're it. In this age, families are long gone from homesteads. Outside our own small worlds, we are anonymous now. Old friends, even brothers and sisters who know us best, are spread across the country. We're suddenly far from the people who knew us in grade school or lived down the street from us. And therein lies the struggle.

We can be anyone we choose to be now. Anyone but ourselves. Which makes social charade—the little lies, the tiny but impressive diamond, the manufactured educational or professional history—so alluring. The truth is that impersonation—the ability to be who we are not—is simply so easy to do now. Which makes the sixth step of humility more important than ever before, perhaps.

To just be ourselves is not so easy anymore. Television and the internet tell us where to go, what to do, what to buy, what we must own, where the action is. To stay common and honest with everyone is not easy anymore. Tattoos tell us who and what kind of person we're talking to, perhaps. Clothing signals a stranger's state of mind and even their status in life. But how much of it is real?

In fact, how much of myself is real anymore? Hoarding things and hiding things in order to create a public image smothers life before it ever starts. When enough is never enough, happiness is always just out of reach and unrest is pervasive.

The truth is that too much of anything erodes its essential power. Too much partying leads to a loss of concentration.

Too much travel leads to exhaustion. Too much makeup distances us from the glow of the natural. Too much self-talk identifies us as narcissists. Too much posturing, too much affect, too much drama leaves us clown-like and alone on the stage of life. There's no one to talk to because few are really sure enough who this person is to risk the interaction.

Indeed, too much of anything robs us of the rest of ourselves. It also cuts us off from others. It separates us out of the crowd, yes, but it can also separate us from the arena of the normal, the nice, the simple people of the world, who mean no harm, who hide no face, who are themselves sterling enough to assure the rest of us of their quality.

The point is that only simplicity can save me from burying myself away from the world in layers of pretense so thick that I, most of all, have no idea of who or what I really am.

The effect of this kind of simple openness to the world is electric. Jesus said of Nathanael that he was "an Israelite in whom there is no guile." He was a completely honest man who did not play at being anything he was not. He was simple, direct, clear. He was what we all set out to be.

The spiritual implications of life lived honestly, openly, simply are overwhelming.

If I am content with less than the latest of everything, I cannot be frustrated by the fact that others have the newer, better version of anything. If what I have does everything I need to have it do, why bother to want it to be bigger and better—unless, of course, it will make me look better than I am.

If I am content with "the lowest and most menial of treatment," I can't be insulted by anybody. Nor, then, will I begin to doubt or despise myself. I know who and what I am. I know of what I am and am not capable. I know what I do well, what I can't do at all. Those who do it all better than I do nevertheless, have no reason to try to humiliate me because I have never pretended to be able to do more.

If I am content with what I have, I can never be ashamed of my clothes, or feel obliged to apologize for my car, or try to hide my house or my furniture again. My mother had this step down to a fine point. When, as the new arrival in town, I was suffering the taunts of children in a new school, she taught me the lesson of a lifetime. "As long as your face is washed and your hair is combed and your clothes are clean," she said, "you have nothing to be embarrassed about."

The demon of self-aggrandizement smothers the rest of the truth in us. We lose contact with what we really are and try to substitute for it what we wish we were.

The sixth step of humility, to be "content with the lowest and most menial treatment," frees us from our false selves. Now we can take life as it comes, full of the personal peace that comes with being relieved of the burden of the superfluous, the inauthentic, the masquerade. It is this kind of humility that is the ground of our growth, the height of our spiritual selves, the best we have to give to the world.

*The Seventh Step of Humility*

# LET GO OF A FALSE SENSE OF SELF

The seventh step of humility is that we not only say but really believe that "we are inferior to all and of less value, humbling ourselves and saying with the prophet: 'I am truly a worm, not even human . . . ' (Ps. 22:7) . . . And again, 'It is a blessing that you have humbled me so that I can learn your commandments' (Ps. 119:71, 73)."

## *What is the challenge here?*

During our novitiate year, the one totally unrelated task, it seemed, was the requirement that we each memorize and be able to recite the entirety of Benedict's Chapter 7, "Humility."

For some reason, we could grasp the fact that this year of almost total cloister—with the exception of four visits from our families—made sense. After all, we were beginning another whole kind of life. Of course, we would need to break ties with the world we'd each come from as daughter, friend, blooming young adult. Yes, the concentration on prayer and domestic duties rather than study and professional preparation was necessary. Being able to spend time on domestic tasks would sharpen our sense of community responsibilities and force a new kind of interior life as well. After all, what else was there to do except clean, pray, and reflect on the magnitude of our decision to seek admission to a religious order that was almost fifteen hundred years old?

Nevertheless, the memorization of the longest chapter in the Rule, with its dense structure, its numerous scriptural citations, and its seemingly unrelated and foreign ideas, was daunting. We struggled through it a line at a time. But if truth were known, it was a dull and dreary task with very little insight gained for all the effort. If anyone really knew what all of this meant, nobody was saying.

To young women of a century fairly exuding sophistication, some of this chapter was at best esoteric. What, for instance, was a passage about laughing doing in something tradition called one of the great spiritual documents of the ages? And worse, why would anyone want us to memorize a passage in which we declared to ourselves, "I am a worm, not even yet human"?

The very thought of memorizing something like that appalled. And, I have learned over the years as I worked with others as eager as I had been to be "spiritual," it appalls at least as much—if not more—today. If nothing else, we had been taught our uniqueness, our potential, our human worth all our lives. And now we were to memorize "I am a worm, not even human"?

Women, in particular, had been living this kind of inferiority in the name of God for generations. Patriarchy, after all, is nothing more than institutionalized pride. Men learn young that they are superior, that women are lesser. That they are leaders and women are to be their followers. That they are the last answer in everything, that women's gifts of mind and soul are to be ignored. So, for generations, the West, which prides itself on its rationality, has ignored both the concerns and the resources of half the population of the world. How healthy was this in an age that had discovered self-esteem?

Everyone in my novitiate had been irreversibly marked by a rising culture of independence and individualism, whatever the standard hierarchies of life and family and community said to the contrary. Of course those ideas of rank and place, of the limitations of natural gifts were all true, we knew. But a new question, in this new era of psychology and personalism, was emerging. How could you have anything stable and strong that didn't begin with individuals who were themselves stable and strong—self-identified and self-directed?

And yet here in the Rule upon which I was planning to base my life, I was required "not only to say but believe" that I was "inferior to all" and of less value. The very words galled even the most pious of us. It was a kind of spiritual schizophrenia. Both positions I knew were true—but one of them, the notion of equality and opportunity, we did not talk about.

I looked to the real world and found ready confirmation. It was the fifties. Everything around me seemed to concur: Such a so-called spirituality of inferiority had to be wrong, maybe even destructive of personal growth. The world had never been better, had it? A globe ravaged by the worst war of all time was now, because of us, over. The world was finally at peace. Evil had been defeated. We were the saviors of the twentieth century.

And then it all began to unravel. One decade at a time.

First, the labor unions erupted in the late 1940s. By the mid-fifties, racism had reared its ugly head again. In the sixties, in Vietnam, in wars of our own era, it was we who napalmed babies. In the seventies, women's liberation, which had begun for this generation in the munitions factories of World War II, made great gains and then broke out in a war against women that is with us still in gang rapes, domestic abuse, victim blaming, unequal wages, and unequal representation everywhere. In the eighties Reaganomics divided the country financially—irrevocably. In the nineties the Middle East became a local, soul-searing issue. In the new millennium, the simmering poor are becoming restless, becoming resistant, becoming refugees, becoming terrorists.

The whole charade of a perfect world with perfect people was crumbling before our eyes. The end of World War II had not brought either national superiority or perfect human community. Someplace within each of us, as well as around the globe, another war, the search for equality—the war we'd ignored—was beginning to seethe.

I began over the years to consider three things I had never before even thought about. First, I wondered, was humility the missing virtue of the modern world, where clamor and competition had become the demons of the time? Second, were women victims of the abuse of humility? And third, was it time, perhaps, as the seventh step of humility says, to admit that we really hadn't evolved into as high a degree of humanity as we had been led to think? What if we really were still inferior, hard as that would be to admit?

Indeed, the memorization of the chapter on humility was only the beginning. Now came years of contending with it, one step at a time. The results turned my cultural formation inside out. My view of the world and the spirituality it needed began to change. Here was a spirituality that started where all the catechism I had ever been taught ended.

Benedict's steps of humility began with the notion that we already had God. I had been taught for years that we had to earn God, however impossible that might be.

I had been taught that the spiritual life is about "becoming perfect." The Rule of Benedict was equally clear: There is no such thing as "perfection." There is only the recognition that God is God and we are not. After that admission, everything else about the spiritual life, the Rule implied, follows in order:

Our relationship to authority figures must be more than mere submission.

The expectations we ourselves have a right to impose on the rest of the universe have as much to do with the needs of others as with our own.

The delusion of grandeur that comes from a sense of entitlement is groundless.

And, finally, our attitude toward others cannot be based on superiority of any kind.

Indeed, little by little I came to understand that the seventh step of humility was written for me.

I, who had declared myself publicly to be a religious, failed always to do it right: either ritual or righteousness. I went to prayer but daydreamed through it far too often. I worked with children and failed to be as compassionate as they were forgiving of my insistence that they be more perfect than I was. I knew all the rules and cleverly avoided many of them. Until then, I had accepted submission of women to men as a synonym for humility and so actually participated in the skewing of human development and human relations.

No doubt about it: The seventh step of humility didn't talk about sweet things like the mystery that is God or the blessing of obedience. The seventh step of humility talked about giving up the arrogant untruth of my white superiority as well as claiming my equality as a woman.

Just as the Rule reminds us, I came to understand that there is no thing, however base, of which I myself am not capable. The anger that ends in murder has a seed in me, too. The deceit that fuels dishonesty niggles at my soul. The arrogance that dares to judge others despite my own pleas for mercy is forever alive and well. They are all proof of the depth of my own need to scale the heights of humility, where honesty will keep me humble forever.

All of the dimensions of Benedictine spirituality, it became more and more clear as the years went by, cascaded directly from the first step of humility. It taught me that the spiritual life is about being willing to immerse ourselves in the heart and will of God. Then, knowing that God is God, we will know just as clearly that we, on the other hand, are only human. More than that, we realize now in the most palpable of ways that we ourselves are clearly capable of anything under the sun.

Why, it was becoming clear, given the humility it takes to accept my own weaknesses, I might someday find enough understanding and even compassion for others who are struggling with theirs.

## *What is the underlying issue?*

In a society that glorifies achievement and success, the very thought of a spiritual life based on what appears to be groundless deference and debasement of self is totally unacceptable. How such a posture might possibly be mentally healthy, let alone socially sound, baffles us. It is simply out of temper with the times. It challenges all the conventional wisdom of the day. It leads to a kind of quiet suspicion of spirituality itself. Why would anyone buy into a philosophy of self-destructive self-doubt? What can anyone mean by such a posture? And, most of all, what good can such a position possibly achieve?

And yet, on the other hand, how can the exaggeration of the self which this society engenders—its moral righteousness, its social inequities, its racism and sexism and genocide, its pathetic self-centeredness, and its ecological indifference—possibly be good for any of us?

These questions about the role of the human in creation have agitated the soul of the world for centuries. History is filled with figures who in their greatness have alarmed us: the emperors of Rome who subjected and exploited one people after another; Alexander the Great, who set out to conquer the whole known world; Christopher Columbus, who plundered and pillaged the new world into the submission of Native Americans to the white West; Adolf Hitler, one of the madmen of our own times, who launched international genocide; Joseph Stalin, who murdered and enslaved millions of his own people; Saddam Hussein, who intimidated and enslaved his country into consent.

But at the same time, history is filled with figures whose greatness of soul has given us hope, has given us models, has given us confidence that the world will not crumble into its own egomania, blustering as it sinks into oblivion: Jesus, who spent his life raising up the poor and abandoned in the face of oppression by both synagogue and state; the Buddha, who taught the world compassion; Francis of Assisi, who confronted ruthless capitalism with the face of poverty; Frances of Rome, a wealthy woman who cared for the poor and inspired other wealthy women to do the same; Harriet Tubman, American slave woman who, at risk of her own life, led other slaves to freedom; Mother Jones, a founding member of the American labor movement; Mahatma Gandhi, who led a people out from under Western domination without taking a single life; Oskar Schindler, who saved the children of the hated Jews in Nazi Germany; Mother Teresa, who brought the attention of the world to the destitute and homeless; Dorothy Day, who called the whole church to deal with poverty and peace.

How do we account for such a stark difference, and what does that difference have to do with the seventh step of humility? Which sense of greatness must we cultivate now, in our own time? What kind of greatness does the seventh step of humility set out to develop?

The distance between these two kinds of greatness is arrogance in all its forms: personal and national. Arrogance is a land beyond a normal and sound sense of self. Narcissism, its extreme, is a sense of superiority on steroids.

Narcissists make themselves the center of the world. And

they expect other people to keep them there. Which means they expect special attention at all times, in all relationships. They keep the focus on themselves at all times. They can— and do—change any conversation back to themselves in order to satisfy their insatiable lust for admiration. Self-centeredness oozes out of their bones. Power is their drug of choice. Grandiosity is their basic behavioral flair and defensiveness their armor. These are people whose empathy level, whose sensitivity and care for others is close to zero, whose shrines are to themselves, who are their own gods.

And we all have a touch of that narcissism.

Which is another way of saying that we can all struggle, at least from time to time, with the touch of narcissism left over in us from childhood and early adolescence. If not noted and checked, our own ability to develop authentic and growthful relationships may well dissolve into the most pernicious kind of self-love, tragic both for us and for those around us.

This disordered sense of self manifests itself from flashes of haughtiness to surges of superiority. It ranges from being dismissive of other people to being totally indifferent to other people's feelings. It begins with boastfulness—the notion that I am better, brighter, bigger than all these other people—and can exhibit itself all the way from pure bluster to a grandiose sense of personal preeminence. It can be a personality flaw or a character flaw. Wherever it arises and whatever it does, it introduces social chaos—forever trumpeting itself like elephants braying in an empty forest, demanding attention, threatening danger.

In an era of ecological ruin, the privileging of the human race—at least some parts of the human race—actually threat-

ens what it sets out to enhance. In such a climate, the seventh
step of humility is a welcome addition to the moral fiber of
the world. It requires us to distinguish between healthy self-
esteem—an honest awareness of accomplishments and personal gifts—and the pathology of self-love.

The narcissist sets out to eclipse the gifts and contributions
of everyone else, and becomes, ironically, his or her own worst
enemy. Such narcissism is grandiosity at its grandest. It stamps
the life out of everything it touches and sucks in all the air
in the room. It is a danger to us all in every category: In religion, it makes itself conscience. In government, it makes itself
a citizen king. In the human community, it sets out to stamp
out competition everywhere, to outshine the entire glistening
world.

It is at this point that humility is its only antidote.

Benedict's chapter on humility, written in a period of de-
cline and transition in Rome, was written for Roman males
in a society that had always privileged Roman males. Benedict saw arrogance and narcissism at the center of the empire
and discounted both. Instead, he began his work of spiritual
renewal by making humility the very heart of his spirituality.
The kind of greatness Benedict offered was the greatness at the
heart of the Gospel. It was a life dedicated to God, to growth,
to peace, and to community rather than to the aggrandizement of the self.

It was an entirely new way of being alive. It takes us to
another level of humanity—the humanity that lives as much
for the development of the human community as for the development of the self. It is at this point that we begin to realize
that as humans we, too, are capable of the worst, "not even

human," as the psalmist says. We come to know, then, in the deepest part of ourselves, that becoming humanely and humbly human, becoming spiritually evolved, is the goal of life.

It is precisely that to which the Twelve Steps of Humility are designed to lead us.

*What are the spiritual implications of this step of humility?*

The seventh step is a kind of crossover point in Benedict's Twelve Steps of Humility. In a way it is this seventh step of humility—the one that brings me face-to-face with myself—that tests the first six.

The progress of spiritual growth in the steps of humility is a slow and steady one. Each step builds on the one before it. Each of them, we come to realize, is another level of depth in our relationship with God and the full flowering of the spiritual self.

The first step of humility brings me head-on with the Divine Center of my life. It confronts me with the ultimate reality: God is God, creator of the universe, and giver of life. All life. The implications are clear: No life, not even my own, can begin and end with nothing else but me and my agendas, me and my hurts, me and my goals.

The second step of humility brings me to plot my path through life—and the direction, if not the route, is plain: If God is God, then the true north of my life cannot be gods of my choosing. We are here for a reason, yes, but we are not here to do our own will. We are here to do the will of God. We are here, in fact, to align our will with the will of God.

The third step of humility brings me to seek wisdom in

others who have gone before. We are brought to accept direction, to be willing to be led, to grow, to develop into more than we are at present.

The fourth step of humility reminds me that the way to fullness of life is long and the path is steep, but that is no reason to forsake it. Endurance itself, the Rule teaches, is an essential part of the process. Every spiritual life has its plains and highlands, its straight-faced mountaintops and deep dark valleys. What is worth seeking, the Rule argues, is worth pursuing to the end. Otherwise, my life can never become what it is really capable of being.

The fifth step of humility urges us to unburden ourselves for the climb. By stripping myself of all the masks and trappings I have collected, I can move more quickly, more freely, more joyfully through life.

The sixth step of humility challenges me to free myself now of hopes for prestige and status, for attention and special treatment. It invites me simply to be myself and to let that be enough for me. It is a call to simplicity and authenticity.

Then, with this seventh step of humility, I am faced with the moment of truth: Indeed, I am "inferior to all." A truth from which we all shrink in horror. And yet, given the time and the social system in which it was written, Benedict's Rule is a spiritual revolution. Both then and now, grandiosity was the climate of the day.

In each of us roars a zero-sum game of superiority that no one wins, but nothing ends it. All the evil such an attitude unleashes only makes the world around us a more dangerous place to be. To consider ourselves to be "superior to any" is to give ourselves the right to dispose of those who are lesser than we, in any way we like.

In our century, those who consider themselves superior assume that they can deport anyone they like from the very visible members of society. They can wall some in or keep others out. They can exclude the ones they call inferior socially and financially. They can write different laws for them according to their sex, their color, their religion.

But only those who know themselves to be inferior to someone somewhere on whatever basis—national standards or social status or intellectual gifts or simple, sheer lack of professional preparation—can honestly understand the pain of exclusion and suppression, injustice and discrimination. Only those who understand the public price to be paid as a result of their own inferiority can bring the balm and the empathy needed to make the human community a community.

The temptation to be faced in reading this seventh step of humility over fifteen hundred years after it was written is to dismiss it as bad psychology. After all, we live in a world of self-esteem. At least some of us do—in some places for some people. The truth is, however, that this step is, at bottom, the best possible psychology. When we believe that we have to be the best, we can never truly be ourselves. And worst, we tend then to overlook—to reject—the gifts and insights of others. We isolate one part of the human race from another.

Benedict wants to form in us the kind of greatness that opens its arms to the world. He wants soulfulness that transcends differences made to be boundaries. He prepares us to give ourselves as bridges to the rest of the world, intent on healing the wounds and divisions of the planet. He wants us to be big enough to recognize and accept the gifts others offer to our own growth.

This kind of humility enables us to take criticism without rage or indifference and so become more than we ever thought we could be. When we are willing to take criticism we are able to learn, to develop, to not only come to know the self but be compassionate with others as well. We know all about hurting now, and so we can finally feel for those who are hurting around us.

Then we are able to admit and to embrace our own humanity. Then we realize that there is no reason for, nothing at all to gain by, playing superwoman or the next male god. When we understand our own limitations, we come to respect the greatness of others.

We can own our own struggles now. No reason to be perfect—since we know finally that there is no such thing. On the contrary. We realize that it is actually the pitfalls we've survived, the pain we refused to hide, that makes it possible to share our scars. And not be scarred again by doing it.

Most of all, looking back on all our angers, all our lies, all our rantings about the sins of others, we now know ourselves capable of the worst. In the spiritual X-ray of the human condition, we have finally discovered ourselves to be the most human, human being of all. Most important, we don't have to deny it anymore.

We have now completed the journey to our own humanity. We are human and know in the face of our own continual struggle to become—to rise as often as we fall—when we see the other struggle, too. "There but for the grace of God go I."

The seventh step of humility is the self-knowledge, the self-acceptance I need to believe in growth and compassion both for myself and for others.

The demon of perfectionism blinds us to the possibility, the necessity of ongoing personal growth.

It is here at the seventh step of humility that we finally learn not to say any longer "That's the way I am." Now we are able to say with great goodwill and certain faith, "There is more that I can become."

*The Eighth Step of Humility*

# PRESERVE TRADITION AND LEARN FROM THE COMMUNITY

The eighth step of humility is that we do only those things "endorsed by the common rule of the monastery and the example set by the prioress or abbot."

## What is the challenge here?

It was the night before Final Profession—a totally life-giving event—and we were all bent over our desks working frantically on last-minute preparations for the ceremony the next day. Every vow paper had been handwritten. Each of them would be signed separately in the course of the ceremony next to the Benedictine Cross at the bottom of the page. I had designed the cross—about the size of a quarter with a blank spot in the middle—to be inked in by the sister after she signed her name. Finally, satisfied with the crisp black of the cross and the precision of its four fanned corners, I piled the papers on the Director's desk to be given to each of us in the morning.

The Director found me just getting ready for bed. She handed me the pile of vow papers and said, "We don't make the cross that way. These will have to be redone." "We don't make the cross that way" was code for "It's not our tradition."

I can argue the point of tradition and traditionalism, of course. Tradition is vital, but traditionalism is nothing more than its weak shadow sister. Traditionalism repeats the past, it considers the past impeccable and so suppresses the development of a bona fide tradition in the present. The distinction between those two approaches stuck for my entire life. There are some things that seem meaningless, perhaps, but that touch the very center of the identity of a people, a culture, a tradition. Determining what those are is the real crux of the problem.

There is a point in life when the last thing in the world anybody wants to hear is directions from someone else, someone older, someone who has been there before. This is our time. This is my life. This is the way I want to do things. The way it's been done before us, has no meaning whatsoever at a time like this. I remember the period well. There were so many people older than we were, all of whom had been trained in a different world, all of whom were intent on preserving it. And there I was, trying to straddle them all—to design a picture of the old cross in a new way.

After all, to be young is to be in the business of finding the self, of developing a voice, of being able to choose, to decide, to strike out on your own. It's all about learning not simply to be yourself but to trust yourself as well. And that may well mean making decisions unlike the decisions other people think you should make. It's about failing at some of them, as I learned that night—and then learning from those mistakes.

It's called the growth process. It's trial and error, try and fail, fail and try again.

The message of the vow papers was clear: To do otherwise than what had been done before us was to fail to live the life as the life was meant to be lived. As it had been lived before this time. As the tradition demanded.

But, if the truth were known, I had already begun to wonder what sameness had to do with holiness. I debated with myself about why these ways were better than the many other ways the same things could be done: like how to hold a prayer book, or the meticulous way to sing the psalms, or how to break dinner bread into pieces small enough to balance my knife and fork. All of which customs were tightly defined.

They seemed to me to be preservation for its own sake. I could not come up with a single sensible reason for not going with the flow of time around us. In this country at least, no one puts pieces of bread under their silverware anymore as we were being trained to do. It was only on a trip to France years later that I learned that when plates were scarce there, pieces of bread were used to clean the diner's dish between courses. Apparently the custom of dividing bread into small pieces was an important European peasant thing from centuries ago. But now?

More than that, such rigid procedures for such inconsequential behaviors tended to lock down the mind. If breaking bread at meals was such a hidebound process, how could a woman ever begin to imagine being something other than a teacher here? In a society in which education had long since become compulsory, would we ever be able to imagine other ways of serving people? The ones wandering our streets now—cold, hungry, mentally limited, and ignored by the system at large, for instance.

Clearly, custom and tradition and sameness had become matters of moral import. Matters that affected the very impact of religious life itself.

I watched women come—wanting to be part of a deeply spiritual, purposeful kind of community life—and go—not wanting the formalism, the rigidity, the relentless conformism that went with it.

So what was this step of humility, which seemed to confirm such a static life? Could it ever have any real meaning in my life? In anybody's life?

It was the tumultuous sixties when the floodgates began to open. The world had apparently reached another one of those moments when its tectonic plates were shifting, knocking against one another, rupturing the earth on which we all had stood for centuries. Now, past ways in almost every discipline or social structure began to give way to new views of what it meant to be alive.

Young American men began to refuse induction into armies that willy-nilly went to war on command. The Vietnam War fractured the national consensus on what it meant to serve your country.

This time it was resistance against marijuana rather than the prohibition of alcohol that divided the generations.

Now young women began to demonstrate for women's

rights again—and pressure for entrance into previously all-male enclaves.

African Americans did sit-downs at government buildings, did sit-ins at white people's lunch counters, conducted voting registration campaigns throughout the South, demanded desegregation.

We were in a national game of pickup sticks. Everything we had thought would be eternally unchangeable had been thrown up into the air and come back down in total disarray.

In the Catholic Church, Vatican Council II ushered in not only the right to question even the fundamentals of the life, the liturgy, the purpose of our rigid practices in both parishes and religious orders, but even the obligation to do so. Tradition and everything it implied about rigidity as a way of life came noisily into question.

Suddenly, everybody came alive. The notion of immutability that had been built into the spiritual life began to crumble. Suddenly there was more to the spiritual life than the repetition of age-old systems, conventions, and customs. We began to imagine a life that was at least as much about adult thinking as it was about childlike submission. To be a woman religious, I could see now, was about being an adult woman in the Church, a real carrier of the faith as well as a consumer of its edicts. We were being invited, in other words, to learn from experience, to value wisdom figures, to follow the path of those who had tried life and found it navigable, whatever its difficulties.

The question, of course, is, What happens when the past is scuttled simply because it reflects the values of ages gone by?

And, conversely, what happens to the present when the past supplants it? What is the effect of change? What is the difference between tradition and traditionalism? The truth is that the entire world is dealing with these questions right now.

Internationalism, technology, communications systems, psychology—every modern discipline stands at the breakpoint between the past and the future. One side of the divide ended with World War II. The other side of the divide began with the nuclear age, the space age, the age of technology, diversity, globalism, and, yes, Vatican II, the council that called the Church to enter the modern age.

The two worlds were alike only in name.

Suddenly nothing looked changed and at the same time nothing was the same as it had once been.

The *Leave It to Beaver* generation, for instance, whose TV series celebrated the nuclear families of working fathers, stay-at-home mothers, and teenagers in sports coats and pleated skirts, simply disappeared when none of us were looking. In a late-twentieth-century world, white supremacy gave way to the Civil Rights Movement, Vietnam protests, ecumenism, and feminism.

No, the notion of family didn't change, but the way we went about being families did: old homesteads disappeared as new families began to spread out across the country, following large corporations from one job to another. Blended families became a new norm. Even the definition of marriage was rethought.

Business, too, was transformed by new theories of leadership and the findings of organizational psychology. Companies got bigger, less local, and workers who had expected to

stay with the same industry until they retired found themselves part of mass production systems. Now central corporate
offices were in another state or even in another country. Employers were distant and unknown figures. Workers, like the
products they made and sold, became just more anonymous
pieces of the process. The voice of the laborer became lost in
the maelstrom.

Populations diversified, communications divided the national mind into multiple perspectives on the same topics, national boundaries gave way to a more porous global internet.
What had been clear and stable national cultures began, with
the merging of East and West, to be multicolored, multilin-
gual, and amorphous.

In the backs of our minds, the categories of culture, our
traditions—family, religion, work, country, neighborhood—
all stood as pillars of society. But the customs, the protocols,
the papal decrees, the structures that once were their glue all
succumbed to new ways of being fathers, mothers, careerists,
believers.

Even churches found that the list of immutables, unchange-
ables, absolutes, and unquestionable canons were, in fact, all
in question.

"It's always been this way" became "We don't do that anymore."

Now the universal question became how to maintain the
essence of each category while none of the old dictums were
still sacrosanct.

After Vatican II shook the nineteenth-century foundations
of the Catholic Church, Catholicism's relationship with other
religions and new definitions of our own became paramount.

We ourselves worked on those questions for over twenty-five years. Trying to determine how to tell the tradition—the essence of Christianity and Catholicism—from traditionalism—the past customs and cultural practices that had come to be considered its essence—plunged the whole community into the depths of theological, psychological, and social development.

But without such periods of history, I realized, every institution on the planet will fossilize, will crumble, or, worse, will go on existing but without purpose. We would become nothing more than artifacts, cultures of empty shells from an earlier age.

Questions like this mark every era of abrupt and total change. They represent crossover points in every society. Every century has negotiated them in one way or another. But now, in our society, they come with an added concern. When change is the new normal, what becomes of long-standing but slow-moving institutions as the world tilts wildly from one side to another?

These questions, I came to see, are important for the spiritual life in a special way. After all, what road to God is sure if devotion and even theology must change to meet the character of a world awash in newness of both data and culture? What spirituality can possibly accommodate the best of the past and still embrace the challenges of the new in such a revolving door of understandings?

These were questions, I knew without doubt, upon which our very lives depended.

## *What is the underlying issue?*

Change at any level, personal or social, is always difficult. Even change that for whatever reason is desired can be destabilizing enough to break the hearts of those who are forced, with little or no involvement on their part, to be part of it. Change, after all, is the journey from familiarity to the unknown, from security to fear, from a history of success to the possibility of failure.

As a result, resistance is inevitable. It is also stultifying. If the urgency of the journey from stability to change is not apparent, if the reasons for change are not persuasive, the hope for change is at best weak. And yet, for anything to remain what it is, it will need at some time or other to change just to stay what it is, to keep up with yesterday, let alone tomorrow.

In the global society in which we live, where people and organizations are daily being shifted from one side of the world to another, change has become a fact of life for individuals and institutions everywhere. In fact, a whole new basement industry has grown up called change management. The purpose of this new network of management, business, communications, and social psychology is to make what could easily disrupt, even destroy, stable institutions as smooth as possible. Where individuals are concerned, it serves as a kind of spiritual and psychological thermometer of the ability to survive change. But the truth is that, however large and established an organization may seem to be, however strong the individuals whose lives have been uprooted, the challenge of companioning people through the process of major change is a delicate one.

The hidden element in change is that it can be done on

paper, by the flicks of pens of those who will be least directly affected by it. At the same time, change can come down hard on the lives of those who are not only the carriers of the institution but in many cases its creators and developers as well.

And therein lies the problem. After the release of the documents of Vatican II, the great effort for change in the Church erupted in a maze of emotional confusion. We struggled with the idea of change in the structures of religious orders. We strained to balance the skewing of perceptions of change among the faithful as well as in the hearts of religious themselves. What would happen to the traditions that gave the spiritual life meaning? In fact, what would happen to tradition itself? Was the past considered useless now? Lost? Simply being abandoned? And at what cost to us all?

Change in the Church and religious life was not about how to manufacture smartphones more efficiently around the world. This change was about how to help people find God in a basically secular or strangely new spiritual world in whole new ways, sometimes even in a whole new language. It meant making a deeply rooted spiritual life new again for another age.

A lifestyle long geared to apparent changelessness found itself dealing with a call to live newly in a new world. The challenge was momentous. Just as the change to women's suffrage shook the secular world, the inclusion of women in discussions on change in their own religious institutions upended the churches. Just as desegregation affected neighborhoods and cities and white supremacy, the thought of religious on the streets with the poor rather than inside religious institutions brought the Church to a whole new way of being.

Just as the country had to find its identity all over again after periods of massive social change, so did we. How to change what had seemed unchangeable, without corrupting the charism, the purpose, that drove it was the issue. How to change what it looked like or how it operated without destroying what it was about at the soul of it, was the spiritual task of the generation.

The outbursts of newness at every level of the faith—clerical, academic, lay, and religious—convulsed the system from top to bottom. What seemed theoretically desirable one day became the fault lines of revolution the next. How much change could the need for change tolerate without bringing down the entire institution with it?

And all the while, the eighth step of humility, to do only those things "endorsed by the common rule of the monastery," acted both as a barrier to change and as the only sensible companion through it.

It was time to wrestle with the difference between tradition and traditionalism in a rapidly changing world. It was a new question in institutions that took for granted that yesterday was a guide for tomorrow. The spiritual importance of the value of tradition was incontestable, of course. But the tendency to make traditionalism—the repetition of a thing simply because it has "always been done this way"—a worthy substitute for tradition was eating like a moth at the threads that made a spiritual life in a modern world possible. It created a built-in tension: the most important one of all.

Tradition is what constitutes the heart and the soul of an institution, its purpose and reason for being, its highest vision of itself and its deepest dreams. Traditionalism includes all the tiny little customs and practices, laws and explanations that reflect the insights important to maintaining that tradition in every particular age that succeeds it.

Jesus of Nazareth became "Jesus of the Galilee" where the needs of the day were most apparent and the concerns of the people least heard. That Jesus had no qualms whatsoever about confronting the tradition with the shortfalls of traditionalism.

As Godfrey Diekmann, monk of St. John's Abbey in Minnesota, told his students, "Tradition is not the stuff we pass on; tradition is the passing on of the stuff." Tradition lives and thrives on the energy and clarity of its vision and its dreams, its purpose and its goals. Traditionalism stands to smother the tradition under an avalanche of time-bound practices that served one generation well but have little spiritual nourishment or meaning to offer the next.

Which is where the eighth step of humility becomes a light in the darkness.

Random change, change for its own sake, change without purpose, can create an erratic society, an agitated life. It jerks us from new idea to new idea with no clear plan in mind. It can be exciting, yes. It can even be illuminating. But whether it can ever bring real substance needs to be an important concern. Otherwise we can find our lives at loose ends, lacking real, deep-down joy or a sense of genuine value, real belonging, a connection to continuing depth and a holy past.

It's change that is undertaken with the tradition in mind that counts. And for that a sense of history becomes a kind of angelic guide through a desert of possibilities. Every spiritual community needs a community memory to help it trace the values and purpose that drove the high and low points of its development. It's not what we did that counts. That's simply traditionalism. It's why we do what we do that is of the essence of tradition.

To be alive is to try things. As John Henry Cardinal Newman put it, "To live is to change, and to be perfect is to have changed often." The reality of that insight is comforting. It is also clarion in its message: We learn as much from our failures as we do from our successes. And that's where Benedict's insight into the spiritual value of the eighth step of humility gives us a lighted path through change: It is the memory of the community—its recollection of opportunities missed; its recall of life-changing risks that catapulted the community into a totally new life cycle of success—that makes change a sacrament of hope.

More even than the memory of its history of change, the model of a community's leaders becomes their legacy to the next generation. Their being able to link past and present and still maintain the quality of spiritual life is what moves us from era to era.

The eighth step of humility liberates us from slavish commitment to the customs of the past. It frees us to move into the light of the Spirit with hope and with faith. Then, breathing the freedom tradition brings, the next period of our lives will be even more attuned to our place in the present than the last. The eighth step of humility frees us to accept the grace of change. It stretches us to go beyond ourselves into the mind of God for the world and to make ourselves a living part of it.

*What are the spiritual implications of this step of humility?*

Groups of any size seethe with ideas. There are as many ways to do a thing in a group as there are people in the group. And that, of course, is the very foundation of creativity. But the successful group is a group with a common mind, a single purpose, a tradition. The proverbial team of horses that pulls in different directions does not pull a coach faster, it simply pulls it apart. In the end, then, it's what individuals do in a group that really shapes the group.

It's the way we deal with change as individuals that will determine not only the effectiveness of the groups to which we belong but the tenor of our own souls. Change teaches us that only the eternal is eternal.

Change affects my identity. What the group is, I am. Until it changes. And then I need to recommit all over again. "Who am I?" becomes a new question at one more disturbing time in life.

Cultural expectations, the ground upon which we stand, shudders, too. What can people expect of me now? In fact, what am I myself willing to promise now? All the old bonds that we thought were set forever begin to pull and creak. People said of sisters who adopted new ways of ministering—soup kitchens, peace institutes, organic farming projects—that they "had left religious life." Except that they hadn't. But it took years before the public realized that the only thing that had changed was the *way* sisters ministered to the world—not the character of their commitment.

Social integration becomes a profoundly serious factor in change. Trying to determine where I'm welcome or what I'm expected to do there now can be as frightening as it is demanding. Knowing where I fit in is essential to my sense of being. The fear of what others will think of me or expect from me or resist in me can shatter people's confidence as well as their longtime zeal.

I met a woman in an elevator one day who was shocked—and upset—that I was a sister who did not wear a medieval habit. How could she tell I was a sister? she demanded to know. "Easy," I said. "Just get all the rest of the women in your parish to wear their wedding dresses. Then, when you see someone in church who's not wearing a wedding dress, it'll probably be a sister." It takes time for a community to redefine itself after great change, but the fresh air of new life is worth it.

At the same time, "we" becomes "some of us," at best, because change is slow. It can take generations for the old to melt into the new. In the meantime, the sense of commonplace and community gets restricted, sometimes even erased.

And yet, what else is the spiritual life but the merger of external growth and internal depth? It is precisely when change separates us from our old self that faith becomes the light in darkness and unity or consensus—real oneness, real acceptance, real understanding—becomes authentic.

Benedictine spirituality is a spirituality with the group mind firmly rooted in the gospels but intent on the development of the community itself. A community, formed in the gospels, stands as a beacon of truth and compassion, of human harmony and spiritual light. In the eighth step of humility, all of those facets of group building are clear.

The models I choose in the community on which to pattern my own spiritual life must be people at the heart of the best of the system. Benedict says quite rightly that our guides need to be those who best embody both the community's future and its past. By tracing leadership images over time, the one arch virtue which, during each period, served to both hold the group together and move it on emerges as a touchstone for the ages. Tradition leads us to find experience tried and true upon which to fashion our own lives and in that way ourselves to influence others.

I learn to live the tradition by watching the others who live here. I remember Sister Margaret, an old gnome who did nothing all day but run supplies to every part of the community. Old cotton blankets to fill the holes in the wires that held our small cots together. New sheets to replace the worn ones. Always with a smile, forever with a blessing. She was herself a model of simplicity. And Sister Pierre, the old Irishwoman who hugged homesick postulants until they could laugh. She showed me that no amount of discipline must ever smother love. Sister Remegia, who made all our clothes out of one pattern and tried to make them fit. And Sister Mary Margaret Kraus, past prioress, who did not think the past "a thing to be clung to," who opened the windows of the community to the changes of Vatican II. They were a treasure house of tradition, the best the spiritual life had to offer.

But not only must we choose models, we must live to become one. Which means that, as much as the community owns us, we must own it. One of the basic spiritual implications of the eighth step of humility is that to benefit from community it is essential to participate in the development of the community. It means that we must help shape the common mind and to participate in its evolution. It is a call to take my place in the fulfillment of the human enterprise, whatever human community I come from—lay, clerical, or religious. Part of my spiritual responsibility is the flowering of the character and quality of my own small piece of the world as that world grasps for new life and grows to new heights and changes. It's then, too, that we begin to look back to the ancestors who brought us this far and cling to their examples of fidelity and hope.

These ancestors, our models, the durability of the tradition bind us together and hold us together from one life-changing question to another. Nothing external can destroy the group that faces its stresses together, open to one another's needs and ideas and refusing to be strangled in the attempts of any smaller part of it to suppress its growth.

Of all the steps of humility, the eighth is the most subtle, maybe, but the most enduring as well, perhaps. Its lessons are obvious: What the group has to give me and what I myself bring to every group will, in the end, be the final measure of its worth. It and I will shape and mold one another. And even more subtle than that is the fact that it is in the holiness of the group itself that we all become holy together.

In the end, then, community is the ultimate test of humility. It's in groups that bullying becomes possible—unless we stop it at its first advance. It's in groups that we learn to listen to others and so make ourselves capable of listening to wisdom beyond our own. It's in community that we begin to see the value and goodness of the others who cherish what we cherish but hope to preserve it in ways different than ours.

The humility inherent in the eighth step is the call to inherit the world of the others. Once we allow someone else's agenda to take precedence over ours, for instance, the world takes one step back from war. We ourselves come to model that strangers can differ, can listen to what may seem to each of us to be a totally different language, can care for something besides ourselves.

Our communities—our churches, our institutions, our cities, our nation—free us from having to reinvent for ourselves all the wheels of life. In every group is the wisdom of the universe. It is simply a matter of wanting to tap into it. In every group is the answer to itself. We don't go to groups to lose ourselves. We go to groups in order to become our best selves while we enable everybody else there to become their best selves, too. We come to groups to find the acumen we ourselves lack and become part of the enlightenment that is at the heart of the group itself.

Our communities are the world in microcosm. It's in them that we can see the value of tradition and the depth of communal wisdom. Groups shake off the dry leaves of the past. They prune the tree of the tradition over and over again so that in every age it lives on.

The Benedictine symbol of Monte Cassino, Benedict's monastery, is a tree. The inscription at its base says *"Succisa virescit,"* cut down it grows again. And so, the order, the tradition, moves on from generation to generation, growing here, being pruned there, always adapting to the soil in which it's planted. And so do we as people.

And all the while, the message is clear: There is no room in a group for rigidity, for the worship of the past, for the fear of the future. It's exactly here where I can myself become this great tradition and seed the future with the wisdom of its past.

Individuals join a community to find the models and support it has to offer. It's there that I can admit my own deficiencies. It's there that I can make up for what I lack by encouraging the growth of others. It's there that I can attach myself to teachers who have been nourished by the acumen of the ages. It's there that I get a close and personal glimpse of holiness alive and flourishing. It's there that I become conscious of the glory of God in others.

The demon of rigidity traps me in my past. Without respect for the holiness of change, my soul will turn to cement, closed to God, closed to the future.

With trust in the Spirit who inspires change in the world, I will become part of sacred change and cocreator of an even better future.

*The Ninth Step of Humility*

# LISTEN

The ninth step of humility is that "we control our tongues and remain silent, not speaking unless asked a question, for Scripture warns, 'In a flood of words you will not avoid sinning' (Prov. 10:19), and 'A talkative person goes about aimlessly on earth' (Ps. 140:12)."

### What is the challenge here?

To be an only child is to deal with a built-in relationship with silence. I'm an only child and, believe me, I know.

Because the only child is alone more often than most other children, silence becomes a natural companion. At the same time, because only children are alone so often, they are unusually eager to talk with peers. Community life is a gift to them, not a problem. As I grew up, I spent a lot of time alone—reading, playing my piano, studying. I loved all of them. I never considered silence a burden. On the other hand, silence was not an obsession either. If anything, I went out looking for friends. Monastic silence, it seemed, would not be a problem for me from either perspective. Which was true, except that monastic silence, I came over the years to understand, was a completely different thing.

The kind of situational silence I lived in was not what this step of humility has in mind. Silence, in the spiritual tradition, is about something more than simply being alone.

Monastic silence is not only about not talking. I learned that one quickly. I was now surrounded by people with whom I would have loved to be able to spend hours of delightful but idle conversation. But in a monastery, I discovered, that was exactly what I was expected not to do.

No, monastic silence is not so much a deprivation of human contact as it is a spiritual exercise the intention of which is to open a sacred conversation with the spiritual self. Our Novice Director was quick to point out that simply sitting down and staring vacantly into space is not a monastic exercise.

But monastic silence does not come either quickly or easily. I remember using silence as a young novice to slip back inside myself. Sometimes I sang silent songs as I did daily chores— either one voice or another of Bach's Two-Part Inventions. At other times, I recited old poetry. Then, eventually, as the pre-professed years went by, I began repeating litanies or mantras over and over again as I went from one task to another. The point was to keep my mind from getting caught up in my studies or my work lists or my lesson plans, devoid of reflection, submerged in the mundane.

Finally, I began to read the *Journals* of Thomas Merton, a veritable mother lode of ideas that had come to him in the midst of a Cistercian silence, the most strict of all. I was looking, I realized, at silence alive, at a living silence that pulsated in my soul surely as much as it had in his. At that moment, I began to understand what "holy" silence, as they called it, was all about. It was about beginning to knead the soul until a whole new life, a new spiritual enlightenment, could rise in it.

I knew then that the silence itself had to be nourished. It did not come out of whole cloth—at least not yet. It came out of the activity of a soul at rest—the very antithesis of noisy silence, busy silence, as I had known it.

Merton was dealing in his soul with the ideas of great spiritual thinkers before him. Struggling to make them intelligible, even debating them a bit. He was trying on those ideas himself. Following them down the paths and crevices of his mind, he began to stretch and pull them this way and that. Out of that reflection the entirely new vision of the life they offered came into view. This, I thought, I can do.

I began to memorize one line a day from the writings of classic or contemporary spiritual writers of the time: Augustine, Teresa of Avila, de Caussade, Janet Erskine Stuart, Eugene Boylan. Until eventually, as the years went by, the words began to come almost entirely from Scripture: "Leave the fig tree one more year. . . . It may bear fruit next year." And "Is not this the fast that I choose: to lose the bonds of injustice . . . to share your bread with the hungry?"

The silence had become troubling, in other words. As silence is supposed to do. It began to stir up things in my soul I had never thought of before: Why were we more punishment-oriented than patient? Why didn't we really share our bread with the poor? Was simply praying for something ever enough?

My life was beginning to change in dangerous ways. Who could read these words and simply go on with business as usual? Who could see the face of Jesus in these words and not die from shame? Silence began to take over my soul.

It was the silence in me that was agitating for change, for authenticity, for—of all things—outspokenness.

I began to look at religious life as it was then structured with a wary eye. For whom were we living this life? For ourselves, it seemed. For our "sanctification" but not necessarily for anyone else's liberation. And what did that mean for all of us?

It was the mid-sixties before the documents came down from Vatican Council II telling religious to "examine their community's initial purpose, the needs of their members and the signs of the times." I knew then, without doubt, that all that silence had not been for nothing. The tradition was correct: Silence is the key to everything.

First, silence teaches us to go down inside ourselves to find real life rather than to reach for it always and forever outside ourselves.

Second, silence provides us with the harrowing ground of the soul. It breaks up the clods of our lives, it roots out the weeds, it levels the rocky ground in which we've grown.

Most of all, it is in silence that we hear our own cries of fear and pain and resistance, which only in silence can really be addressed. In silence we come to know ourselves. Then, we are ready to disengage ourselves from the thickets that block the way beyond ourselves where light is and growth is and God is.

Silence, I knew now, confronts us with the hardest question of them all: What are we hiding from that our flight into noise holds at bay?

## What is the underlying issue?

It is very easy to valorize silence. Who isn't looking for eternal peace and quiet? But the fundamental challenge of it remains: Why do I want peace and quiet so desperately? What kind of silence are we talking about? Are we talking about the kind of silence that enables us to escape the pressures and truths of our lives? Or is silence the way we control or ignore the people around us? The answers to those questions, Benedictine spirituality implies, are among the most important answers of the spiritual life.

Silence has two dimensions, both of them intensely godly. No one talks about it much, but silence is not only a spiritual discipline. Silence has as much to do with what it means to be a life-giving part of the human community as it does with what it means to be piously reflective.

No amount of talking can ever do as much to bring us face-to-face with ourselves as immersion in our inner darkness. The understanding of the role of silence in life has a great deal to do with how each of us grows and what we can eventually become. Most of all, the way we use silence as a spiritual gift has something to say about our own role in the growth and development of others, as well.

Each of these dimensions of silence—internal and social—determines how we go through life and whether or not we do it well.

The silence of the heart, that deep-down awareness of what we're thinking and why, is our monk's cell. It's in that place of total honesty where we come to realize who we ourselves really are. We learn there what we fear and what we are resisting. We hear there the voices we so commonly block out with noise that seduce us to give in to ourselves. It's in silence that we hear the sounds of our better angels calling us to rise above our lesser selves. It's in silence that we arm-wrestle our picayune selves to the ground of truth.

Silent reflection throws us back upon ourselves, exposes our wounds, and challenges us to authenticity. Silence is not an event—not a confession, not a miracle. Silence is a process that transforms us from an etching of our potential to the fullness of ourselves. Silence frees us from our public selves and steeps us in our spiritual selves so that we have more to give to the rest of our world in the future.

Silence can, of course, become our private game of escapism. We can begin to substitute feeling holy for being holy. We can withdraw from the real world and call withdrawal a spiritual life. We can use silence to avoid the world, its problems, and our responsibility to them. We can simply dissociate from the people around us and tell ourselves that we have done a holy thing. But if we do, we are misusing silence, debasing its spiritual value, and making ourselves our own god, whom we go inside ourselves to worship.

The ninth step of humility is clear: Silence is not for its own sake. The silence we seek is the silence that does not sin the sin of eternal agitation. It is a silence meant to help us—once healed of our anger, finally harmonious and serene—see that the world around us is a graceful and peaceful place.

It is only this kind of silence, calmed and calming, that knows how to listen to others rather than freeze them out in tacit anger or ignore them in the interests of our own self-protection. Silence can become such a holy way of being unholy at our very base.

It is only by listening that we get to really know the other as well as ourselves. The attention we give to others by showing interest in their interests or fears or preoccupations is the beginning of human community. It requires us to actually attend to another rather than simply use the encounter as an excuse to talk about ourselves alone. It is the holiest of human acts.

The understanding that we bring to others comes out of the understanding of ourselves that our own self-reflection has earned us. Only when we know ourselves—our motives, our struggles, our fears—can we reach out to the other without judgment, with care.

It's by listening to the pain and fear of the other that we prove the compassion we like to think we have. It is in the genuine care we bring to the other out of the honesty of the self that wisdom emerges. Both ours and theirs.

In silent listening, one soul is able to meet another without the noise of a garrulous and superficial world to drown out what is trying to be said. It is silence that leads us both to honesty and to insight unalloyed. Then we learn in a whole new way how listening is a dimension of silence and silence is the only ground from which real listening can possibly spring.

Finally, it is silence that teaches us, as the ninth step of humility insists, that there are simply some times when silence is the only real answer that counts.

As the Rule reads, "In a flood of words you will not avoid sinning" (Prov. 10:19). Too often so-called conversations or discussions become arguments and deteriorate into pure folly. No one really gets heard and nothing is resolved.

When comments are made out of anger or spite, meant only to hurt or to bait another person, when no real conversation or genuine, heartfelt communication is being attempted, silence is the only possible answer.

When what I say will only escalate someone else's anger or when what they say is only meant to goad mine, holy silence saves the day and the soul of the relationship.

When what is being said is said with malice, no matter how "true" it may be on one level, truth has not failed us, we have failed truth. When nothing is changing in the attitude or openness of either party, it's time for self-reflection. What is it in me that has brought this encounter to this point? And, more important, I must discover in silence what it is in me that is needed now to put it back together again.

Silence is good when it is teaching me about me and urging me on to become even more of the best of myself. Silence is good when I am listening to the other intently and bringing balm and strength to what could otherwise become disheartenment and demoralization. Silence is good when I refuse to sin with my tongue. And silence is always good when it is the monk's cell to which I go to hear the voice in me that is divine, that is calling me to holiness.

Silence grows me and frees me. It saves me from arrogance and disdain for others by being the place where I go to discover myself. It enables me to become the ear of God on earth, listening for pain and healing it, listening for my own smallness and rising above it, listening for the voice of God urging me always on.

*What are the spiritual implications of this step of humility?*

It was barely dawn. The sun was coming up over a sea rolling with whitecaps—intense but not angry. Down at the edge of the water, she was sitting with her back to me, hands up, head tilted into the light. It was a profile of profound peace and eternal centeredness. It filled her with a kind of stolid serenity. And, it raised my heart and mind to God as well.

Silence does that. It centers and calms the entire world.

The spiritual implications of the ninth step of humility go deep in the human soul. They bring to consciousness the underlying meaning of the spiritual life. Spirituality is not about feeling good about ourselves. It's about doing good wherever we are. It's about bringing good to everyone. It's about becoming the good we seek. It's about fashioning our souls in the kind of silence that enables the whole world to feel safe in our calm and quiet presence.

The ninth step of humility reminds me that the missing spiritual resource in modern society is an appreciation of the role of silence in life. We all live overwhelmed by noise. The human experience of silence gets slimmer by the day. Boats plow our waterways with boom boxes on their bows. Cars squeal past our homes with windows down and belching sound far into the night. Sound sanctuaries are few and far between in a world of canned music, the ubiquitous television, horns and whistles, and airport runways in the middle of the countryside. And all the while, we forget that the spiritual life, the reflective life, starts in silence and grows in silence and comes to fullness in the self that listens to silence.

Most of all, we forget, if we have ever known, that silence is the bridge to humility. To be able to be silent when what we want to do is to erupt into full voice and full force with everyone around us is the essence of humility. Then the world becomes a placid, saner place because we have been there, attentively but quietly.

Humility invites the world into our thoughts and nourishes our understanding with the ideas the rest of the human race brings to us. The humble person does not pontificate at the expense of everyone else who has something to say but nowhere to say it. In those situations, silence is the great equalizer, the forerunner of a genuine democracy.

Humility makes the powerful accessible to the powerless. There is no reason to fear the powerful who are dedicated to hearing those who seek to speak to them. Nor is there any reason for revolt because our ideas—which are all we really have to give—have not been made welcome.

In an interesting twist, silence—the willingness to hear—itself empowers the powerless; it levels the playing fields of the world. It raises up the lowly just as Scripture says and gives them both stage and audience.

Indeed, silence is the great teacher of us all. In the silence within us, we hear our own pain. We plow our own growth. Most certain of all, we bring new hope to those around us. Now, perhaps, they can feel more secure in their own futures because they see at long last that the powerful are as dedicated to the communal voice as they are to their own.

Our moments in reflective silence expose the adversaries

within to ourselves so that we might come to terms with them. It makes us known to ourselves so that we might understand the struggles and needs of others better. The fact is that people resist silence and so run from it as if it were a scourge. And yet, it is only by nourishing serenity within us that we can possibly survive the noise around us, which muddles our minds and stirs our blood to the point of inanity.

It is in the ability to be self-reflective that we can come to think our way through the impulses that drive us to a more tender, more gentle, more meaningful way to live.

Without doubt, silence gives us the power to respond thoughtfully rather than foolishly, maturely rather than out of furor run amok. It teaches us to stop focusing on our own ideas and concerns and attend to the concerns of our wider and more basic purpose on earth.

It's by personal reflection and by listening to the ideas of others that, in the end, we begin to grow to full stature. It's in silence and listening to others that we learn self-control, kindness, and compassion. None of these ideas come packaged. They come only through experience: the experience of my own struggles and the awareness of the soul-stretching experiences of others.

We learn in silence that our struggles are not either the center or the fulcrum of the world. They are simply the compass point at which we come to understand the strife and trials of others and our own call to alleviate them.

Ironically enough, it is silence—self-reflection and listening—that makes a person an honest citizen of the world. Once we acknowledge our own demons, we become a genuine member of the human community. We can stop lying to ourselves now about who we really are. We can stop plunging headlong into the fabricated cacophony of a world trying to hide from itself. We can even stop trying to hide from ourselves, because, having found ourselves, we no longer need to go on attempting to be someone else.

Finally, we know that talk without thought is not only useless but destructive of relationships, of truth, of possibility, of the very center of our souls. The demon of the ever-chattering self makes me deaf to the voice of God within me.

The ninth step of humility frees us from making a shrine to ourselves. It connects us. It refuses to allow us to cut ourselves off from the part of creation we were born to bless with our openness. It is through a listening silence that we ourselves gain wisdom from the words and ideas of others.

Silence frees us to learn, to become, to reflect, to respond, and to repent. It is the degree of humility that opens us to the entire world.

*The Tenth Step of Humility*

# NEVER RIDICULE ANYONE
## OR ANYTHING

The tenth step of humility is that we "are not given to ready laughter, for it is written, 'Only fools raise their voices in laughter' (Sir. 21:23)."

### *What is the challenge here?*

Of all the steps of humility with which I found myself faced in the early days of my religious life, not one had as much effect on me as this one. This directive against laughing I simply could not accept. Everything in me rebelled at the thought of being at the mercy of a bloodless, humorless existence all the rest of my life—and that in the name of holiness.

I did my best to make up excuses for it in my mind, trying to hang on, waiting for someone, anyone, to declare it officially null and void or at least to modify it. But no explanation ever came. We just read it year after year, without comment, without edits.

When I look back now, that in itself was the only saving dimension of it. No one talked about this one: not in the books, not in religion class, nowhere. Everyone simply ignored it. And, truth was, the community itself was a very funny place.

There was a lot of laughter to be gotten in a monastery just watching one character after another doing very serious things in very hilarious ways. Sister Hildegund, for instance, was stone-deaf. Or so she said. She went shouting through the basement of the monastery, grumbling to herself, totally unaware of how loud she was being in a house committed to silence. Thundering along the stone passageway, she was giving orders to anyone and everyone in sight who might listen. But no matter whether they listened or not, she just disappeared into the rest of the cavern, grumbling about them instead.

"Who's supposed to feed the cat?" she shouted at the novices one day. "She's starving." I don't think so, I said to myself. She's the biggest cat in town. "You jackrabbits!" she said to every novice within earshot. "Don't you know a hungry cat when you hear one? Just listen to her crying!" So much for being stone-deaf! Of course we laughed. And so did every professed sister in earshot.

Or there was the time when a professed sister, one of the dignified and proper kind, bowed over in chapel a bit too enthusiastically. As the community bowed and the prioress intoned the last psalm, we heard something crash on the hard tiled floor. The novices who sat in the front pews watched in horror as a bright new set of false teeth went swirling down the polished middle aisle straight and fast as an ice hockey puck. The entire community stopped praying in midair. Then, in a silence that echoed from wall to wall, the community coughed itself out of chapel, laughing all the way. And no one said a word. No corrections were given. No imperfections spoken during Chapter of Faults that week. Nothing at all. Clearly, this step of humility had fallen off the books somewhere.

*humor*

Or there was the night five fire trucks showed up in the community yard after midnight, sirens blaring, ladders being cracked open, thousand-watt lights moving across the building searching every nook and cranny of the building's face, nuns running madly down the halls, trying to figure out what kind of national attack had hit the sleepy neighborhood of Ninth Street. Until a window opened on the third floor and the prioress leaned out through the wooden shutters, dressing gown flowing and head scarf askew. She was waving madly at every fireman in sight. "No, no, no!" she hollered through the roar of the sirens. "We're not on fire. I just put red lights on the windowsills to scare away the pigeons!" But by that time, everyone else on the block was awake, too. All of them laughing.

We were a community that knew how to have a good time. We had big German pretzel sandwiches on feast days and singalongs on bus trips. We sat around at night and told funny stories from our classroom experiences during the day. We laughed for years about the first grader who stood up straight after he got his polio shot, pointed at his rolled-up-shirtsleeved arm, and said to his nun-teacher, "Just wait till the parents hear about this!"

We reveled in telling public jokes about our jubilarians,

older sisters celebrating milestone anniversaries, at the community dinner every year. And, to tell you the truth, at their memory services after they died, too.

What's more, to this day, six decades after I entered this community, we gather almost every year to hear one of our members do a stand-up comedy routine on the daily foibles of the group. The laughter can be heard halfway into town.

No, we were not—are not—a dour group.

So what was going on? Was this tenth step of humility real or not? And if it had been expunged from the book, why didn't anyone simply say so? And if not, why not?

For someone like me, who collects stories and tells them with relish, the question was an important one. Was this really a community I could be myself in, in fact, be happy in? Or, better yet, was this spirituality emotionally well balanced?

And furthermore, what did laughter, legal or not, have to do with humility?

I spent a good deal of time just trying to figure out why laughter would be considered a threat to the spiritual life. Was spirituality the suppression of life rather than the fulfillment of life, as I had always thought it would be? The question deserves an answer in a world on the brink of grim at all times.

"Only fools raise their voices in laughter," the Rule quotes from Sirach. It was a scriptural prescription, a note, and therefore a weighty one. So, it seems, this step of humility has something to do with fools, with people who are not sharp-witted enough or cultured enough to do differently. This was, at least, the beginning of an answer.

Clearly this step has as much to do with a certain kind of person as it does with a certain kind of action. It's about the foolish, about people who stumble through life, making one hapless mistake after another. The thought is intriguing: Raising our voices in laughter, then, has something to do with making the wrong choices in life. And then thinking it's funny. Like: Drunk is funny; dense about what we should be smart about is funny; doltish is funny. I was beginning to understand. Not to raise our voices in laughter as fools do had to be warning us not to think that bad decisions are meaningless, that bad judgments are amusing to anyone.

I began to understand that there are some things in life that must be taken seriously at all times.

The light dawned: The tenth step of humility means to free us from going through life uncaringly, thinking that all of life is one big joke. Because if we do, in the end the joke's on us. Only those who are too proud to think they can make a mistake or have yet to pay for the consequences of it would think that doing nothing worthwhile is laughable.

## What is the underlying issue?

The Novice Director did not like laughter at all and reserved a very special frown for it. The Scholastic Director, on the other hand, loved a good story but never, ever, laughed out loud. Never, ever, made a sound, however surprising or raucous the occasion. She just stood there, eyes twinkling, mouth open in silent pantomime of good humor and hearty response. A kind of Santa Claus ho-ho-ho without a voice box.

And so the question lingered and became even more irksome as the years went by: Why, in so profound a document as a Rule for monastic communities written in the sixth century, had laughter occupied such a prominent place in the very cornerstone chapter of its spirituality? And, frankly, how psychologically healthy could a person—or a community—be without laughter?

Interestingly enough, I discovered, the history of laughter in societies and religion is a rich one. No novice director had ever traced the relationship for us, but the association was very clear.

Indeed, laughter had a great deal to do with the early disquisitions on humility. Yet over the centuries, the meanings attributed to laughter came to be understood differently. In later cultures, the subject remained just as important as ever but with more spiritual, sometimes even mystical, overtones.

Clement of Alexandria, the first Christian theologian to treat the subject of laughter, was not so much intent on eliminating laughter—which had long been the basis of satire and religious mockery in Rome—but to constrain it. He was committed to the notion that reason ought to dominate the emotions but that laughter disturbed reason. Laughter, he argued, is an outburst that violates rational communication. Even smiling, he taught, had to be bridled.

The ongoing teaching for centuries thereafter took the position that excessive laughter is a sign of a weak and undisciplined character. It undermined human dignity, the theologians argued. The early leaders of the Church, to a man, inveighed against it. Ambrose, Jerome, Basil, and John Chrysostom—who pointed out that Jesus never laughed—all of them considered laughter the anteroom to lust. Laughter, they said, was centered in the body, polluted the soul, and so crowded out the Word of God.

Tradition had spoken clearly: Laughter was a first step on the road to eternal doom. And chief among all conclusions was the notion that monks and hermits, above all, were to weep over the miseries of the world and concentrate on the suffering and death of Jesus. Not spend their lives in inane laughter. One religious Rule after another warned against the role of laughter in distracting the religious from the important things of life.

The teaching was well established long years before Benedictine religious life appeared on the scene. Christianity had already conquered the "eat, drink, and be merry" philosophy of the Roman Empire. Life now was about salvation, not sensuality, not "bread and circuses." Five centuries before the Rule of Benedict, rigorous rationality had already put down deep roots.

In the thirteenth century, however, Thomas Aquinas began to interpret games and mirth and even John Chrysostom's teachings on laughter differently. Then, in the fifteenth century, the philosopher-priest Marsilio Ficino pronounced laughter to be "gracious." It was a clear break with tradition on the subject and signaled an entirely new approach.

Finally, with the later recognition of the positive value of the human body, a new conversation began on the necessary role of laughter, propriety, beauty, and Divine Joy. These medical and psychological insights changed the trajectory of human development and continues to this day.

In fact, laughter, in our time, has become big business. There are claims aplenty made for it at the highest levels of medical and scientific research. Emphasis on laughter's place is now a firmly established meme in the quality of human relationships, social bonding, emotional health, stress reduction, and physical health. The pictures of our grandparents—he seated, she standing behind him, both of them stern-faced and unsmiling—have given way to laughing women and rollicking men whose laughter comes off the pages of our photograph albums in waves.

So, now? What now for us and our generation, and especially for our spirituality? Has the tenth step of humility been declared defunct? Is there any use or meaning to it? Can it possibly be an adequate bearer of so great a spiritual concept as humility?

The answer to all those slivers of the problem is a simple one: It all depends on what kind of laughter you're talking about. The laughter considered irrational that focused the first fifteen centuries of this spirituality? Or the kind of laughter that has to do with scorn and derision, with disdain and disparagement, which also borders on the irrational, that is so much a part of our own experience?

In this century, laughter is not a universal sign of lust or a loss of rationality. And yet, the way laughter is used as a weapon now can be far worse. Candidates can get elected to high public office by hurling verbal insults at their competition in the hope of reaping a harvest of malicious laughs. In ruination politics, the reputations or good names of other candidates are reduced to sneers or snickers. The favorite indoor sport of today's howling public is to urge the political lions in the electoral arena to snap and snarl and bloody one another. No doubt about it: Rationality is long a thing of the political past. And so of our political maturity, our public participation, of the spiritual depth of civic society, as well.

If this step of humility teaches us anything, it is that humor and laughter are not the same thing. Benedict does not forbid humor; he forbids the bawdry and the brutal. He makes the quality of our laughter a measure of our spiritual adulthood.

Fools, he says, quoting Scripture, "raise their voices in laughter." Fools: the dull and the unwise, the imprudent and the silly, the demeaning and the sarcastic. Once we ourselves fall into the habit of deriding others, we join the ranks of the foolish, too. And why would any of us do that? Surely only because we have not owned our own afflictions, our personal impairments, our interior disadvantages, our clear and public impediments. It's only when we face our own shortcomings and personal limitations that we stop laughing, sneering, or snickering at anyone else's ever again.

Then, humility frees us from the burden of insufferable pride. We know now that life is to be taken seriously. This is weighty stuff we are about. The care of the planet and respect for the animals and love for our brothers and sisters for whom we have responsibility are not to be taken lightly. There is no room for foolish, destructive, demeaning laughing anymore. There is no regard for the kind of laughter that is mean and nasty, lewd and lascivious.

*What are the spiritual implications of this step of humility?*

Interestingly enough, the easiest way to discourage a relationship is not to smile at all. We've all known the type. They're straitlaced and serious. They command attention and enjoy control just by doing nothing that looks inviting or fun-loving or emotionally open. What they need, we think as we try to deal with them, is a good laugh. A bit of fun in life. The chance to let down and let go and let be. And that kind of experience, in our own lives, in a world over fifteen centuries away from this call to humility from the sixth century, is proof of why laughter cannot be taken lightly.

We know now that the way we deal with laughter has a lot to do with the way we treat the rest of the world.

Maybe no other step of humility is quite as clear about what it means to have an inflated ego as this one. When we put ourselves in a position to deride others, we have abandoned all pretense at spiritual ripening. Self-knowledge withers and self-control goes to dust. We have lost our tether to the earth, to our humanity, to humility in its fullest, richest meaning.

Humility is not false modesty. Nor is it false humor. Humility owns its reality. Humility is our ability to be comfortable with both the truth of who we are and the truth of who we aren't. The truly humble do not permit themselves to act like playground bullies who taunt others in order to assert their false sense of superiority.

Instead, laughter is meant to refresh our view of the world. What we laugh at gives us new insights into ourselves. It helps us to see what engages us, what has us by the soul—the limitations of others, loveless sex, nativism in a pluralistic world, money and power unlimited? Or love and fun and play and care and joy? We have the chance when we laugh to assess the nature of our laughter. We can now determine its place in our spiritual as well as our social life.

Laughter is meant to heal us, not to divide us from one another. Division is always a sign of the dwarfed soul, the heart that has yet to grow up enough to care for someone besides the self. When what we laugh at divides the world into insiders and outcasts, it is our own souls that are sick, not theirs.

Holy laughter saves us from self-centeredness. It teaches us to laugh at ourselves, not others. It reminds us of who we really are—down deep and hidden from sight. It exposes us to ourselves just in time to save us from making useless shrines to ourselves.

I remember a poor, crippled boy in the neighborhood, disfigured and slow. He ran with a loping limp, groaning and moaning as he went, and I watched the older boys make fun of him, mocking and groaning as they went. Soon after trying for weeks to be accepted by them, he didn't come out to play anymore. He disappeared from sight and hid from those of us called "normal." But the truth was, I knew, even at that age, that those who mocked him were really the crippled ones. His disfigurement stayed with me all my life. Without him I might never have found the soft spot of the soul in me. I should have told him that, but then I was only nine years old myself, and greatly in need of the opportunity to feel ashamed at all the ill-gotten laughter he brought us.

I learned then that thinking seriously about what we laugh at saves us from taking the herd mentality for granted, helps us to watch who we imitate, to be careful who we call friend. We need, as we grow, to be conscious of the kinds of things we laugh about. We need to learn to ask ourselves who won't find the joke funny. Why? Because we need to decide if we want our humor to be our own or are simply going to borrow our laughs from the gracelessness of people around us.

It's an important moment in the spiritual life the first time I stand solemn-faced in the midst of a laughing crowd, too committed to the God of Love to laugh at the unlaughable. After that, I remember to think through the so-called funny things of life one more time, to give them the serious attention they deserve.

Laughter is a very important dimension of life. Because it masquerades as the harmless and the frivolous, it is easily dismissed. And yet what can possibly be more spiritually important than the way we insert ourselves into the world around us? Was Kristallnacht fun in Germany? Was looting fun after the New Orleans flood? Did any of the rock throwers think it through later? Did any of them change as a result? And if not, what kind of a world did we become because of them? Is leering and sneering at women the real stuff of comedy? And, when we see pictures like those now, what happens to our own view of the world?

The spirituality of laughter is running underground within us. It tells us what we do with our rage and what we do with our honor. It refuses to allow us to hide ourselves behind hostile remarks. It makes us think again before we say, "Oh, I was just kidding! Don't take everything so seriously!" We know now what a living lie bad humor can be.

Finally, the spirituality of laughter calls us to protect the powerless around us as well as to deepen our own souls. Until we discover the difference between wit and sarcasm, between what's funny and what's crude or rude or unkind, we have a soul without sensitivity. Healthy humor is what enables us to relate to the rest of the world without threat, without pain. It takes us into the heart of the other and leaves them feeling better than they were when we got there. It gives the gift of holy laughter, which takes away the gloom, the darkness of the day, and makes life alive again.

The gift of humor makes a hard road smooth and a long road short. It brings the world together; it never sets out to tear us apart. Those who give the world a good laugh leave it in better mental health than they found it. They are the physicians of the soul. They enable us to carry our burdens with more energy, more heart than we can ever do in a world that is cold and dark.

In this tenth step of humility, Benedict wrote his sixth-century concern for being rational, reasonable, righteous people. What could be closer to the notion that we must not allow our best selves to be defeated by insulting or bullying everybody else? The spiritual point of the tenth step of humility is that humility walks through life softly, kindly, caringly, and with a dignity that refuses to stoop to pornographic laughter. And because of it, we are all better, all kinder, all happier—all freer, all more full of the love of life.

The demon of mockery exposes my own emotional neediness. For those whose laughter is crude or lewd or unkind, there is no such thing as spirituality.

For those whose laughter is kind and life-giving, the heart is already open to the universe. For them, laughter is the sound of the presence of angels around them.

*The Eleventh Step of Humility*

## SPEAK KINDLY

The eleventh step of humility is that "we speak gently and without laughter, seriously and with becoming modesty, briefly and reasonably, but without raising our voices, as it is written: 'The wise are known by few words.'"

### *What is the challenge here?*

It didn't take long before we all figured out that the "war to end all wars" (World War I) didn't end war at all. Instead, peacetime became a bridge from one war to another, all of them deadly, all of them fruitless. The government whipped up support for them by inciting fear of communism, and the churches concurred.

In fact, the society found itself slipping into a culture of war—one after another: Korea, the Cold War, Vietnam. Then Afghanistan, Iraq—the Middle East, the debacle no one saw coming. It was a time of eternal conflict. A time of tension and uncertainty like no other. The answer to everything, it seemed, was violence.

We were in one conflict after another. And this time the violence spilled over into our city streets, into our children, into our schools and inner cities and small towns. Into our DNA.

In the monastery some years later, I tried to imagine what kind of world the writer of the eleventh step of humility had known. It had been a pretty bucolic place, I supposed. At least until I knew a bit more about the Roman Empire and its fall, the persecution of the faith and its martyrdoms, the collapse of social order and the takeover by the barbarians—the foreigners and immigrants of their time.

And yet, in the midst of that kind of upheaval, the writer of this Rule called for measured tones and gentle words. More than that, he called Roman men, of all people—the privileged and the powerful—to live gently and kindly, humbly and reasonably. Amazing.

How realistic, I wondered, was such a proposal either there or in my own country, in my own time?

Then, one day, I came across a study that turned my head around completely. It said:

The medieval monarch Frederick II (Holy Roman Emperor, 1194–1250 C.E.), was alleged to have carried out a number of experiments on people. These experiments were recorded by Salimbene di Adam, an Italian Franciscan friar, in his *Chronicles*.

Frederick II, Salimbene di Adam recorded, carried out a deprivation language experiment. Young infants, he decreed, would be raised without human interaction. That way, he thought, he could determine if there was an innate natural language that would emerge in them once their voices matured. Frederick was seeking to discover, Salimbene said, what language would have been imparted unto Adam and Eve by God.

Salimbene di Adam wrote that Frederick encouraged "foster-mothers and nurses to suckle and bathe and wash the children, but in no ways to prattle or speak with them; for he would have learnt whether they would speak the Hebrew language (which had been the first), or Greek or Latin, or Arabic, or perchance the tongue of their parents of whom they had been born. But he labored in vain, for the children could not live without clapping of the hands, and gestures, and gladness of countenance, and blandishments."

And so, all the children died. The point made by such a cruel experiment may not have suited Frederick II, but it, and so much of contemporary social psychological research, has much to say to us. First, communication is part of the life force that drives us, shapes us, brings us to fullness of life. But, second, perhaps just as important, the way we communicate will determine the quality of our own lives as well as of the lives of those we touch.

But I didn't really need academic studies to prove the truth of these points. I have traveled a great deal in a world where international contact and "citizen diplomacy" have become standard. And I have learned the hard way that language is the key to all of it. The night I was stranded in the mountains of Italy and minutes away from the last bus back to the city was excruciating. I had no way to call a cab, no way to ask for help, no way to find lodging in the dark. Why? Because I had no way to make my needs clear.

Or the day in Egypt that I could not find my way out of the bazaar and back to our cab because I could not read the Arabic street signs, or storefronts either for that matter, let alone read a phone book to make a call.

Or the day that the train we were on went on strike and left us on the siding, too late to catch our train to Switzerland and no way to get reservations for the night.

The examples are endless. I can still feel the fear of it all, even in the attempt to tell the stories. We are a people of mixed tongues trying together to build a better world. And what can substitute for the languages we do not have?

Never has understanding been more significant than in our own time. The globe is a chattering, blathering polyphony of languages now. A veritable Tower of Babel. Each of us speaking our own language, often at cross-purposes with the language next to us.

What we say and the way we say it now has the power to destroy the entire world. The very thought of it brought me to a great pause in life. For the first time, I stood in actual awe of a document, sacred in its wisdom, holy in its intent, that can speak to us from the sixth century with such clarity, such simplicity, such overarching wisdom. The eleventh step of humility is as pertinent as this morning's news.

I began to see as never before that, at base, life is about language. Our own, first, must be gentle, reasonable, brief, and modest. Humble. We are not the ruling center of the world. Most of all, we must learn to listen. Then, we must learn to speak with all the needs of the world in mind. And wherever we are, in whatever family, church, city, society, country, we must take the first step toward a loving, peaceful world by speaking there as we would want the entire world to talk to one another.

We must begin to free the world from this perpetual war of words by freeing ourselves from the acrimony our own words can bring.

## What is the underlying issue?

The interesting thing about the eleventh step's approach to humility is that, unlike the tenth step, on the nature of laughter—which at first glance sounds so arcane—this one sounds so modern. So contemporary. So natural. We are, after all, a communication society that only midway through the twentieth century discovered the quandary and quagmire of interpersonal communication and set out consciously to decipher it. To discipline ourselves to the canons of it. After all, we have finally learned that on communication, almost totally, lies the future of human relationships.

This step of humility leaves no doubt: Holiness has as much to do with building community as it does with developing a routine of pieties. We are the sum total of what we do to others, for others, because of others. The way we speak to one another, this step makes clear, makes us look at ourselves as well as at our attitude toward people around us. If we bother to look at them at all.

For most of recorded time, communication was a series of formal dos and don'ts—do wear white gloves in public, do help women out of carriages, do show deference when speaking to an authority figure by lowering your eyes, do bow to some and nod to others. Every slight manner of speaking or relating to others was concerned with propriety rather than personalism. And most of even those things were practiced almost exclusively in high society, not among peasants and commoners, whose lives were more a matter of survival than social nicety. The eleventh step of humility, then, was far ahead of its time, far more about being humane than about merely being proper. This was a function of humility meant to bring people together in mutual respect rather than divide the world across a chasm of false obedience, false respect, false differences, and false emotions.

The other interesting factor in this step is that it was written first for monastics—vowed and professional religious—in a society more accustomed to hermitages than to communal religious life. Which means that Benedictine spirituality gives as much attention to talking as it does to silence. There is, then, inherent in Benedictine community living the concept that community is built on relationships, not simply on living alone together.

Finally, this step of humility requires the very basics of what contemporary social science calls "interpersonal communication." Speech in a Benedictine monastery, we're told here, is expected to be gentle, kind, serious, modest, brief, reasonable, calm, and emotionally controlled. Or to put it in more current professional terms, it is to be intentional, purposeful, relational, open, and mutually satisfactory.

Most of all, this step is a bold, bare instruction in human relationships. It's not about giving orders. It's not about exercising authority. It's not about demonstrating our power or our intelligence or our public status. This step is simply and surely about what it takes to develop human community. To be clear: There is no step of humility that deals with the way we are to do our work. No, but there are several about how we are to live with one another—strangers though we may, to some extent, remain for all our lives.

We are to be clear about what we need from one another. There is no place in human community for hinting at things or manipulating people. We are to be direct but kind. Always kind.

We are meant, in fact, to engage with one another, to listen seriously to one another, to realize that life is not all about us. What's even more clear is that good communication must never be all about us. Good communication listens. And then it responds in ways that make this interaction as good for the other person as we want it to be for us. It reaches out to the other. It discovers then what it is to have someone else reach back with the same amount of care and sensitivity we first gave them.

Good community life does not engage in baiting one another. We work together in order to get good things done well and at the same time to be friends to one another as we do them. Our communication is intended to create harmony— peace and equality—among us. But that can only be done by caring as much for the person whose help we seek as for the work we are about to do together. However good the work may be, it can never outweigh what happens to people emotionally as a result of the climate we create as we do it.

We do not lord it over one another. We are modest, this step of humility says. We are reasonable and calm. We are adults who know how to manage our own emotions and are keen to be sure that we do not incite another's emotions at the same time.

This step gives us a clinic in what it means to be relational, to understand another person's stake in the conversation. We are not to approach anyone with difficult or injurious words meant only to showcase our own power to make someone else's life miserable.

Most of all, we are to deal with one another calmly and reasonably—no dispensations from civility given for age or professional standing or position and title. The older may not intimidate the younger; the professional may not deride the staffers; the ones with titles of any kind are not allowed to give orders and nonnegotiable commands to those who carry the weight of every day.

It is a call for what Daniel Goleman—now, centuries later— calls "emotional intelligence," the kind of self-awareness that saves others from our sharpest tongues, our cruelest barbs— the parts of ourselves still to mature, not quite under control. It calls us to realize that emotions are a communicable disease. We catch them from one another, but we are each responsible for our own.

We must come to understand that our darkness can eclipse another person's sun and so refuse to allow that to happen. The negative energy we create can undermine an entire group. It is our responsibility to create the rapport between us, the kind that makes a good family great, an institution a positive addition to society, an effective community a beacon of light to many.

I got it: In a hostile world, the eleventh step of humility frees us from seeing ourselves as the center of the universe when actually it is really all about everybody else.

## *What are the spiritual implications of this step of humility?*

In some ways, the Rule of Benedict is much more bold about its definition of humility, of sanctity, than most of the spiritual language we've become accustomed to in recent centuries. It is a plain-speaking, real-time look at what makes for holiness. To Benedict the spiritual life is not a philosophical discussion or a theological treatise on the difference between spirit and matter.

From the first line on, the Rule of Benedict brooks no distancing nonsense, not a scintilla of an idea that holiness is about anything but the presence of God and the will of God for humankind in all things. The path is clear: Know that God is in the here and now. Don't talk about earning God. You have God.

What follows after that, then, is simple: Remember that only God is God. The word *humility* itself—meaning "of the earth"—makes the point. We are not to make ourselves gods, a relatively common practice for rulers in the empire. Our role in life is to do God's will for humankind. We are not to despotize anyone else, however privileged our origins. We are not to oppress anyone else, however powerless they may be.

The eleventh step of humility, one great dimension of which requires being gentle, being reasonable, being serious about life, leaves no doubt about the way we are meant to go about the human enterprise. And, most significantly, it is all within our grasp. It's all about the way we live life and, most important, about the way we treat others. It's about human community. It's about what the twenty-first century needs most right now: a way to live well with those near us and a way to live well with the rest of humankind at the same time. We are here to build the kinds of community where everyone is equal, everyone is worthwhile, everyone is safe from ridicule and rejection.

In the eleventh step, the simplicity of it all is overwhelming. Speech, we learn here, is a gift. Speech is a tool of sanctity.

Holiness is not about hiding from the world in the depths of our rituals or in our distance from the questions of the time. On the contrary, the Rule plunges us into the great issues of life—human community, simplicity, equality, self-control, and now into something as basic, as all-encompassing, as the way we talk to one another. There is no promise here of being able to buy our way into heaven with a string of pieties. On the contrary. The spiritual life, the steps of humility imply, requires a great deal more than that. It requires that we attend to the needs of others as well as we do to our own.

When we join the crowds calling out for the torture of our enemies, where is our gentleness then? When we applaud plans to export poor people back to their poverty so that we can all be richer as a result, how reasonable is that? When we expect special treatment for ourselves but ignore it for others, how modest, how humble, is that?

The truth is that egoism—the idea that my world begins and ends with me—is the bane of community. It warps and distorts the very soul of humanity. It makes those who shout the loudest the leaders of the pack. It abandons the basic principles of human community: relationship, interdependence, equality, and care. It is a barren spirituality that begins and ends with me.

Oppressive speech—sarcasm, rebuke, anger, abuse, derision, defamation—drowns out love and splits the world in two.

Human unity or world division begins with what I say to people and about them. To other nations and about them; to our enemies and about them; to our competition and about them; to our wounded, our hangers-on, our outcasts; to the little ones of our world. It's the way we talk to the other that determines how much peace we ourselves bring to it. "Love thy neighbor" is, in the end, all about what I say to the rest of the world and how I say it.

Narcissism, on the other hand, deliberately sets out to make other people invisible, to suck up all the air in the room, to absorb all its light. But the eleventh step of humility repeats to us again and again that the others are there waiting for our care, not our censure or our curses.

One of the most poignant, most meaningful of the sayings of the Desert Monastics for our time is the story about an abbot and a peasant. Abbot Arsenius had a well-deserved reputation as a holy man, a learned man, a scholar, and an ascetic. He was rightly exalted and revered. The peasant spent his life cultivating his farm on the banks of the Nile as it flooded and receded from year to year. It was a difficult and largely thankless task, yet in its simple way maintained the community around it.

One day, the story goes, Abba Arsenius was asking the old Egyptian man for advice about what he was thinking. But someone overheard the conversation and said to him: "Abba Arsenius, why is a person like you, who has such a great knowledge of Greek and Latin, asking a peasant like this about his thoughts?" He replied: "Indeed, I have learned the knowledge of Latin and Greek, yet I have not learned even the alphabet of this peasant."

The eleventh step of humility is not about playing at being nice to people whom I would otherwise normally not even notice. It is about coming to realize the real worth and skill and gift to humankind of every person I see.

It's about beginning to understand that every person we meet is a gift of wisdom to us. We have something to learn from each of them. And we have something everyone we meet needs from us: a sense of value, a deep-down respect, a genuine admiration, a recognition of their contribution to the world.

The demon of idolatry ensnares us in a spiritual life whose boundaries are ourselves.

The eleventh step of humility frees us in a very obvious way from falling into the trap of really believing that we are, at least, our own idol—even if no one else's.

*The Twelfth Step of Humility*

## BE SERENE, STAY CALM

The twelfth step of humility is that "we always manifest humility in our bearing no less than in our hearts, so that it is evident at the Opus Dei [prayer], in the oratory, the monastery or the garden, on a journey or in the field, or anywhere else . . . and constantly say in our hearts what the publican in the Gospel said with downcast eyes: 'I am a sinner, not worthy to look up to the heavens' (Luke 18:13)."

### What is the challenge here?

The message we got as small children in first grade was short and sweet: Stand up straight, put your shoulders back and your head up; place your thumbs along the seams of your skirt or pants; and speak up! And it worked. Even the exercise itself elevated little people to think of themselves as bigger ones.

Years later, during a speaking engagement in England, a

nun at the coffee break rushed up the center aisle to ask me "a personal question." Those kinds of conversations always give me pause. People can ask anything in public after you give them permission like that. "Is it true," she said almost conspiratorially, "that in America every child must stand up straight to answer a question?" I thought for a moment. "Yes," I said, "as a matter of fact, it is true. We teach our children in first grade to stand up and speak out." She nodded her head gravely and turned to look at the small cluster of people behind her. "You see?" she said to them. "That's why Americans are so much bolder than we are." I paused. Bolder? I thought to myself. If she only knew. Even after years of public speaking, I can still wilt at the thought of it.

Nevertheless, however national a mask it may have been, the American invitation to dignity, confidence, and self-assertiveness went deep. Year after year, grade after grade, the message got more and more ingrained. There was a way to carry yourself that had as much to do with who you wanted to be as it was about who you really were—in the back of the mind and the center of the soul, where it really mattered.

The message never changed: If you failed to stand up straight and speak out, you would be marked as a weakling. If you went through life bowed down and simpering, you'd never do anything of value. Behavior like that could only leave you looking like the wounded one in the pack. It would label you as one down, less competent, less ready, than the others around you. And before you even got started. If that wasn't the message they meant for me to get, that's the one I got anyway.

And yet, here, in a monastic setting that I hoped would be my life forever, I suddenly found myself having to deal with what seemed to be exactly the opposite message: Keep your head bowed, your eyes down—"everywhere, at all times, in all places." Now what should I do?

There was a way to walk here, too, and a way to sit. A way to climb stairs and a way to walk down them—emphasis on *walk*. Keeping all the stipulations felt like putting on a suit of clothes that did not fit. That maybe would never fit. It seemed to be one whole way of life on a collision course with another very different one. How would I ever reconcile these two approaches to life, if ever?

It was a simple thing, this tension over how to walk down stairs, and yet it was the very struggle with it that got my attention first, that eventually changed the way I went about the rest of life. My basic inclination had always been to run first and walk later, to get wherever I was going before anyone else or at least not far after them. Speed was my trademark. Do whatever was to be done and do it quickly. Then, get on to everything else. Squeeze the most life out of everything quickly and then rush on to taste the rest of it. My favorite song was the White Rabbit's song in *Alice in Wonderland*. I found myself humming it often: "I'm late. I'm late. For a very important date. No time to say hello. Goodbye. I'm late, I'm late, I'm late." I had no time for what I thought was only propriety.

Yet, as the years went by, I got deeper and deeper into lectio, into reflective reading, and the Divine Office, and the very concept of contemplation. None of which could be hurried or packaged in small, short bites. The daily practice of simply stopping life to allow the soul to explore its essence rather than its externals opens up a Life within a life. With no particular end product expected from it, no mind-numbing number of prayers "to get in," no checklist of special liturgical behaviors or postures to learn or exercises to complete, contemplation deepens us. It is immersion time for its own sake. It is a steeping in ideas, in Presence, in personal growth. It takes us beyond the accidentals around us to the very reason for our existence. Then, eventually, it changes us.

Slowly, quietly, over time, I began to understand what the twelfth step of humility has to say to a world that lives on image building. In a Madison Avenue, image-making, Photoshop society, the twelfth step of humility is a challenge to be who we say we are, no more, no less. In contrast, this society supplies the masks that make for a lifelong masquerade. They imply that pretense is more important than truth.

The twelfth step of humility is, I began to understand, a challenge to turn appearance into authenticity.

To "manifest humility in our bearing no less than in our hearts" requires us to become real rather than try to simply look good. It's about knowing what it means to be true to ourselves. It enjoins us to admit what happens to our souls when we take up life in a never-never land of pretext and charade, of artifice and veneer.

And if we spend our lives lying to ourselves, disguising ourselves from the world, what kind of depth of soul can we ever possibly develop? When will anyone ever see in us the real depth, the total vision, the arc of honesty we so desperately wish could be acceptable to the rest of the world? Hiding is such a strenuous occupation.

The twelfth step of humility is an invitation to come out of camouflage. It prods us to discover that the love and acceptance we seek can only come when truth comes. Then the amazement at being accepted for who we are, under the skin, behind the inflated titles, despite the money, will be the euphoria for which we wait.

Clearly, the question under the question is the ultimate, the final one: Who are we really?

## *What is the underlying issue?*

Who are we now? The answer to that one is: We are the only ones who really know.

Psychologists have been struggling for years to find the key to personal disintegration. What kind of stress is it that can collapse the very structure of a person's life? What is it that threatens to unravel a personality, a commitment, a marriage, a goal? What is it that splits a person in two? Almost without a sign. In an instant. Apparently without warning.

There are multiple reasons, of course—prolonged tension, sudden trauma, anxiety in the present, fear of the future, whatever it is that threatens the security of the self. But, in the end, it all comes down to one: For some reason, under some circumstances, people simply discover that their own sense of self, their previous definition of purpose in life, the feasibility of their goals, the sextant of their lives has failed and fractured somewhere along the line. Like a dual-focus camera, where clarity of the photograph requires that both sides of the subject come into perfect alignment, at least one part of the subject has shifted. One part of the soul is no longer in alignment with the other half of the person. One goal is out of line with the other. One segment of the soul has lost its sense of direction.

Or to put it another way, one or more tiers of the healthy personality—physical foundation, personality traits, goals, or self-concepts—for whatever reason, are out of line with the others. What the soul whispers in our ear that must be achieved does not excite the heart. What the mind believes, the soul questions. The vision the psyche needs before it can proceed with the task of becoming whole has simply evaporated. Goals that were once sharp are now blurred in the midst of turmoil.

It is these built-in dichotomies that the twelfth step of humility calls into consciousness. The twelfth step is the final, but unfinished, task of life. It is the culmination of what the first eleven steps of humility seek to develop in each of us.

The issue that the twelfth step of humility confronts us with, then, is the question of integration. Let's call it the *And so?* question of life. You have immersed yourself in the twelve steps of humility all your life: And so? What has changed in your life as a result?

Humility, this wisdom chapter from the sixth century, is a guidebook to personal integration. The twelfth step of humility is the final test of the success of the process. We are, it teaches us, always and everywhere to "manifest humility in our bearing no less than in our hearts." We are now, as this generation has become fond of saying, to "get our act together." We are not only to recite, to preach, to profess the humility to which the long, slow climb up this ladder has brought us; we are to have become it. The twelfth step requires us to look back on this territory of spiritual development and ask ourselves pointedly and particularly, And so?

1. You say you have learned now from the first step of hu-

mility that only God is God and you are not. And so? When you get up in the morning, how will that affect what you do today?

2. You insist that you understand the second step of humility, that God's will will always be better for you than your own self-centered demands. And so? What did you do differently today as a result?

3. You realize that by accepting the third step of humility, the guidance of wisdom figures, you not only profit personally from their experience but acknowledge your mortal limitations. And so? In what way do you make decisions differently now than you would have before you accepted their role in your life?

4. You affirm in the fourth step of humility that the willingness to endure even difficult things is a sign of faith and trust in God. And so? Through what have you persisted and what happened as a result of it?

5. You maintain in the fifth step of humility that being willing to acknowledge your own mistakes liberates rather than crushes the soul. And so? When have you admitted your bad steps and from what were you freed as a result?

6. You claim in the sixth step of humility that it is possible to be content, to be happy, with less than the best and even in the face of bad treatment. And so? How have you reacted when you were overlooked?

7. You contend in the seventh step of humility that putting down all the trappings that lead to a false sense of self relieves a person. And so? From what have you freed yourself? And why?

8. You think with the eighth step of humility that people should go on learning from people who are models of the tra-

dition even as they age. And so? What have you learned from others in your community, family, congregation, workplace? What did you learn about yourself? What did it change in you?

9. You suggest in the ninth step of humility that it is better to listen, even when you know that you know the answer. And so? Have you ever discovered something by listening that you did not find out simply by talking to another person?

10. You hold with the tenth step of humility that ridicule of differences is wrong. And so? How do you deal with people whose mannerisms irritate you? What do you do differently now?

11. You say you really believe, as in the eleventh step of humility, that it's better to speak kindly, even under difficult circumstances. And so? What have you taught yourself to do to calm conversation in tense situations?

12. And finally, in the twelfth step of humility, you believe that it's important sometimes simply to stand by and let other people take over, talk first, give the orders, get the credit. And so? What happens to you when you do these things? Or, better yet, who are you now as a result?

Humility does not chain us to a lesser self. Ironically enough, it is humility that stretches us beyond ourselves. Humility does not say, "I can never succeed." It says, "Whatever happens, I must always get up again. I must learn to live with failure. I must go on." Why? Because failure is one of the great teachers of life.

The hard truth is that humility is a lesson that can take a lifetime to learn. Yet, in the end, its great reward is contentment, serenity, trust, and a sense of the success that comes from having arrived at the fullness of the self by understanding our own smallness.

Humility is the great liberator in life. No one and nothing can undermine the humble person's confidence in God. Nothing can deter us from committing ourselves to the will of God for the world. Nothing can convince us to adapt ourselves to a world whose greed is crushing and whose arrogance is smothering. We will be forever happy with what we have. We will not live pretending to be what we are not, forever worried that our masks, our toupees, our cosmetics and costumes will come off in public. Everything we do will speak of kindness, of acceptance, of care for those in whose presence we stand. We will have put down all the trappings that are meant to hide our real selves from the world. Freed from all pretensions now, I will be honest, open, and my authentic self to all people and in all situations.

It is the work of a lifetime, yes, but it is a lifetime that gets quieter, calmer, kinder, and more satisfying as we go.

An old monastic tale says it all. The disciple asks, "What do you do in a monastery?" And the old monastic answers, "Oh, we fall and we get up. And we fall and we get up. And we fall and we get up again."

*What are the spiritual implications of this step of humility?*

Mahatma Gandhi wrote, "Happiness is when what you think, what you say, and what you do are in harmony." Gandhi could have been a Benedictine. The twelfth step of humility is about living an integrated life, a life in which each part is in harmony with every other dimension.

What we think, what we say, and the way we go about life cannot be well lived when they are in opposition to one another. When, in fact, they simply cancel one another out, there is no integrity left to any of them. The person who lives a lie, for instance, no matter how effective otherwise, is in tension every moment of the day. The person who pretends to be something they are not—wealthy, credentialed, in emotional control—cannot function openly anywhere at any time.

The truth is that we are meant to be transparent. People, hearing what we say, should know what we think. Seeing what we do with our lives, people can infer what we care about and how we think about things. If we say one thing but think another, somewhere, somehow it all begins to seep out. Worst of all, the burden of hiding exhausts a person from the soul on out.

Benedict in the chapter on humility is quite direct about the intertwined life of soul, body, and emotions as the measure of integrity, strength, serenity, and freedom. In the twelfth step of humility, his clarity is so simple it is stunning. He writes: Our humility "is evident at the Opus Dei, in the oratory, the monastery or the garden, on a journey or in the field, or anywhere else."

The directions are achingly pure: Be what you say you are. Do not lie, even to yourself. Don't live two lives—loving parent/missing parent; honest employee/cheating employee; devoted public servant/self-absorbed public servant. The truth is that egotism is the bane of community building. No one can build anything that lasts when the materials are bogus.

Benedict has brought the steps of humility to an acme in the twelfth. Physical appearance, he warns us, betrays the quality of our souls. People know by looking into my eyes whether I am really intent on being with them or not. They can tell if I am interiorly what I purport to be exteriorly. Even in a culture whose penchant for casual long ago broke the boundaries of either propriety or integrity, excess in any direction says more than I want to admit.

Most of all, what we wear and how we carry ourselves define us. Our clothes, our gait, our accessories—the big signs of religion or the heavy makeup, the overdressing or underdressing, the self-serving boasting or the simple truth telling—all expose us. They add up to what's most on our mind, how honest is our speech, how caring is our presence.

At the end, three things measure both our integrity and the harmony of our own lives: self-control, respect, and freedom from self-deception.

Self-control is the key to spiritual development. To be too much or too little of anything in one dimension of my life creates imbalance in the other dimensions as well.

Respect for other people not only measures my humility but opens me to the wisdom around us as well.

Freedom from the demon of self-deception gives me the chance to go on growing just when I think I have reached my height, plumbed my depths, and know it all. The demons are behind me, the way ahead is open, the self becomes an eternal enterprise in process.

Then, at the height of the ladder, three things happen: First, we look back and realize that the journey has not been a series of exercises. It has been a process of slow and soul-emptying transformation. We find ourselves involved in an entire reorientation of the self—away from the exhausting demands of narcissism to the softening and holy-making ventures of humility.

Second, we see that the change in our mind-set and demeanor have enabled us to relax into the arms of God. Life ceases to be a sprint to an imaginary finish and becomes a stroll through Mystery. We know now that everything in life is not under our control. So we learn to do what we can and then settle into allowing ourselves to take life as it comes. At that point life becomes more an adventure than a threat, more a ride steering through the rapids than a collision with the rocks.

Third, we begin to realize that we have been saved from our driving, pounding, teeth-grinding selves enough to enjoy the rest of the adventure called life, learning, becoming, growing as we go.

The essence of Benedictine spirituality, a spirituality of growth in God and in human community, is a ladder that is grounded in the presence of God and reaches up and out beyond itself to concern for the world in which we live.

Humility, Benedict teaches, turns things upside down. In the spirituality that developed in the Middle Ages onward, life was a series of ecclesiastical dos and don'ts and rooted in pious exercises. When done well enough and regularly, these spiritual duties merited, were guaranteed, to end at the summit that was God.

Benedict's chapter on humility topples that kind of spiritual merit system. He calls instead for a way of life that begins with awareness of the presence of God and is lived with honesty and care for the people around us. It ends at the peak of human community.

Benedictine spirituality is rooted in life—normal, committed, love-giving, life-giving life. "Our body and soul [are] the sides of this ladder," he says, "into which our divine vocation is to fit the various steps of humility as we ascend." If we want to be holy people, people steeped in God, people who have integrated the spiritual and the material in life, we must "climb [this ladder] by the humility of this present life." This ladder of humility begins with God and ends with care for the rest of the world. The two sides of the ladder, he says, are body and soul. The implications of that single statement say it all. This spirituality is not escapist, is not body denying, is not self-centered, is not otherworldly. This spirituality stretches us and points us toward others, to the Infinite.

It is a way of life, a spirituality, a compass point to God. It is life-changing and life-giving.

The steps of that great ladder are definite and distinct. The Twelve Steps of Humility are, at every pace of the way, one step closer to a life that is full of the fullness of life. Brimming with love of God, a proper love of self, and love of the humanity to which we give our care, we are finally authentic and fully free, totally authentic and driven by the spirit of God.

The Twelve Steps of Humility are an invitation to freedom. If they had been written today, they would have sounded very much like this, perhaps:

1. Recognize that God is God.
2. Know that God's will is best for you.
3. Seek direction from wisdom figures.
4. Endure the pains of development and do not give up.
5. Acknowledge faults and strip away the masks.

6. Be content with less than the best.

7. Let go of a false sense of self.

8. Preserve tradition and learn from the community.

9. Listen.

10. Never ridicule anyone or anything.

11. Speak kindly.

12. Be serene, stay calm.

Do all these things and you will achieve that Love that casts out fear in awareness of the Love that is God.

Humility is the ancient secret of life, a spirituality for all time, an awareness of God that plunges us into God's presence in the present moment. Always. The decision is ours.

Finally, fourth, we discover in the last paragraph of Chapter 7, on Humility, a promise that takes us all by surprise. It is, in fact, the only guarantee in the entire Rule. Nowhere else, no other segment or topic of the Rule, ends with any kind of spiritual assurance whatsoever. Here, though, after the slow, soul-stretching challenges of the Twelve Steps of Humility, a promise lies in wait for us.

If we ever wanted a kind of confirmation of the joys inherent in a life that is more centered in the interior life than in the secular goals of status, accumulation, and power, this must surely be it. This paragraph in the Rule of Benedict reads clearly and solemnly, with certainty and eternal promise:

"Now, therefore, after ascending all these steps of humility, we will quickly arrive at the 'perfect love' of God which 'casts out fear' (1 John 4:18). Through this love, all that we once performed with dread, we will now begin to observe without effort, as though naturally, from habit, no longer out of fear of hell, but out of love for Christ, good habit, and delight virtue. All this God will by the Holy Spirit graciously manifest in us now cleansed of vices and sins."

Say it again and again and again: We will quickly arrive at the perfect love of God which casts out fear. We will know the God of Life. We will be at one with the mind of God.

"All that we once performed with dread, we will now . . . observe without effort . . . out of love . . . good habit, and delight in virtue," the passage rings out. It is a breathtaking promise.

The struggle is over now. The demons are quieted. We have come full circle from a search for God based in fear to finding God without effort, out of love, good habit, and delight in virtue.

Welcome home to the arms of God.

*Appendix*

# THE RULE OF BENEDICT:
## CHAPTER 7

*Humility*

Sisters and Brothers, divine Scripture calls to us saying: "Whoever exalt themselves shall be humbled, and whoever humble themselves shall be exalted" (Luke 14:11; 18:14). In saying this, therefore, it shows us that every exaltation is a kind of pride, which the prophet indicates has been shunned, saying: "O God, my heart is not exalted; my eyes are not lifted up and I have not walked in the ways of the great nor gone after marvels beyond me" (Ps. 13:1). And why? "If I had not a humble spirit, but were exalted instead, then you would treat me like a weaned child on its mother's lap" (Ps. 131:2).

Accordingly, if we want to reach the highest summit of humility, if we desire to attain speedily that exaltation in heaven to which we climb by the humility of this present life, then by our ascending actions we must set up that ladder on which Jacob in a dream saw "angels descending and ascending" (Gen. 28:12). Without doubt, this descent and ascent can signify only that we descend by exaltation and ascend by humility. Now the ladder erected is our life on earth, and if we humble our hearts God will raise it to heaven. We may call our body and soul the sides of this ladder, into which our divine vocation has fitted the various steps of humility and discipline as we ascend.

The first step of humility, then, is that we keep "the reverence of God always before our eyes" (Ps. 36:2) and never forget it. We must constantly remember everything God has commanded, keeping in mind that all who despise God will burn in hell for their sins, and all who reverence God have everlasting life awaiting them. While we guard ourselves at every moment from sins and vices of thought or tongue, of hand or foot, of self-will or bodily desire, let us recall that we are always seen by God in the heavens, that our actions everywhere are in God's sight and are reported by angels at every hour.

The prophet indicates this to us, showing that our thoughts are always present to God, saying: "God searches hearts and minds" (Ps. 7:10); and again: "The Holy One knows our thoughts" (Ps. 94:11); likewise, "From afar you know my thoughts" (Ps. 139:3); and, "My thoughts shall give you praise" (Ps. 76:11). That we may take care to avoid sinful thoughts, we must always say to ourselves: "I shall be blameless in God's sight if I guard myself from my own wickedness" (Ps. 18:24).

Truly, we are forbidden to do our own will, for Scripture tells us: "Turn away from your desires" (Sir. 18:30). And in prayer too we ask that God's "will be done" in us (Matt. 6:10).

We are rightly taught not to do our own will, since we dread what Scripture says: "There are ways which some call right that in the end plunge into the depths of hell" (Prov. 16:25). Moreover, we fear what is said of those who ignore this: "They are corrupt and have become depraved in their desires" (Ps. 14:1).

As for the desires of the body, we must believe that God is always with us, for "All my desires are known to you" (Ps. 38:10), as the prophet tells God. We must then be on guard against any base desire, because death is stationed near the gateway of pleasure. For this reason Scripture warns us, "Pursue not your lusts" (Sir. 18:30).

Accordingly, if "the eyes of God are watching the good and the wicked" (Prov. 15:3), if at all times "the Holy One looks down from the heavens on us to see whether we understand and seek God" (Ps. 14:2); and if every day the angels assigned to us report our deeds to God day and night, then we must be vigilant every hour or, as the prophet says in the psalm, God may observe us "falling" at some time into evil and "so made worthless" (Ps. 14:3). After sparing us for a while because God is loving and waits for us to improve, we may be told later, "This you did, and I said nothing" (Ps. 50:21).

The second step of humility is that we love not our own will nor take pleasure in the satisfaction of our desires; rather we shall imitate by our actions that saying of Christ's: "I have come not to do my own will, but the will of the One who sent me" (John 6:38). Similarly we read, "Consent merits punishment; constraint wins a crown."

The third step of humility is that we submit to the prioress or abbot in all obedience for the love of God, imitating Jesus Christ, of whom the apostle says: "Christ became obedient even to death" (Phil. 2:8).

The fourth step of humility is that in this obedience under difficult, unfavorable, or even unjust conditions, our hearts quietly embrace suffering and endure it without weakening or seeking escape. For Scripture has it: "Anyone who perseveres to the end will be saved" (Matt. 10:22), and again, "Be brave of heart and rely on God" (Ps. 27:14). Another passage shows how the faithful must endure everything, even contradiction, for the sake of the Holy One, saying in the person of those who suffer, "For your sake we are put to death continually; we are regarded as sheep marked for slaughter" (Rom. 8:36; Ps. 44:22). They are so confident in their expectation of reward from God that they continue joyfully and say, "But in all this we overcome because of Christ who so greatly loved us" (Rom. 8:37). Elsewhere Scripture says: "O God, you have tested us, you have tried us as silver is tried by fire; you have led us into a snare, you have placed afflictions on our backs" (Ps. 66:10–11). Then, to show that we ought to be under a prioress or an abbot, it adds: "You have placed others over our heads" (Ps. 66:12).

In truth, those who are patient amid hardships and unjust treatment are fulfilling God's command: "When struck on one cheek, they turn the other; when deprived of their coat, they offer their cloak also; when pressed into service for one mile, they go two" (Matt. 5:39–41). With the apostle Paul, they bear with "false companions, endure persecution, and bless those who curse them" (2 Cor. 11:26; 1 Cor. 4:12).

The fifth step of humility is that we do not conceal from

the abbot or prioress any sinful thoughts entering our hearts, or any wrongs committed in secret, but rather confess them humbly. Concerning this, Scripture exhorts us: "Make known your way to the Holy One and hope in God" (Ps. 37:5). And again, "Confess to the Holy One, for goodness and mercy endure forever" (Ps. 106:1; Ps. 118:1). So too the prophet: "To you I have acknowledged my offense; my faults I have not concealed. I have said: Against myself I will report my faults to you, and you have forgiven the wickedness of my heart" (Ps. 32:5).

The sixth step of humility is that we are content with the lowest and most menial treatment, and regard ourselves as a poor and worthless worker in whatever task we are given, saying with the prophet: "I am insignificant and ignorant, no better than a beast before you, yet I am with you always" (Ps. 73:22–23).

The seventh step of humility is that we not only admit with our tongues but are also convinced in our hearts that we are inferior to all and of less value, humbling ourselves and saying with the prophet: "I am truly a worm, not even human, scorned and despised by all" (Ps. 22:7). "I was exalted, then I was humbled and overwhelmed with confusion" (Ps. 88:16). And again, "It is a blessing that you have humbled me so that I can learn your commandments" (Ps. 119:71, 73).

The eighth step of humility is that we do only what is endorsed by the common rule of the monastery and the example set by the prioress or abbot.

The ninth step of humility is that we control our tongues and remain silent, not speaking unless asked a question, for Scripture warns, "In a flood of words you will not avoid sinning" (Prov. 10:19), and "A talkative person goes about aimlessly on earth" (Ps. 140:12).

The tenth step of humility is that we are not given to ready laughter, for it is written: "Only fools raise their voices in laughter" (Sir. 21:23).

The eleventh step of humility is that we speak gently and without laughter, seriously and with becoming modesty, briefly and reasonably, but without raising our voices, as it is written: "The wise are known by few words."

The twelfth step of humility is that we always manifest humility in our bearing no less than in our hearts, so that it is evident at the Opus Dei, in the oratory, the monastery or the garden, on a journey or in the field, or anywhere else. Whether sitting, walking, or standing, our heads must be bowed and our eyes cast down. Judging ourselves always guilty on account of our sins, we should consider that we are already at the fearful judgment, and constantly say in our hearts what the publican in the Gospel said with downcast eyes: "I am a sinner, not worthy to look up to the heavens" (Luke 18:13). And with the prophet: "I am bowed down and humbled in every way" (Ps. 38: 7–9; Ps. 119:107).

Now, therefore, after ascending all these steps of humility, we will quickly arrive at the "perfect love" of God which "casts out fear" (1 John 4:18). Through this love, all that we once performed with dread, we will now begin to observe without effort, as though naturally, from habit, no longer out of fear of hell, but out of love for Christ, good habit, and delight in virtue. All this God will by the Holy Spirit graciously manifest in us now cleansed of vices and sins.

Three versions of the Rule of Benedict have been used in this book:

*The Holy Rule of Our Most Holy Father Benedict Translated from Latin*, Rev. Boniface Verheyen, OSB, The Abbey Student Press, St. Benedict's College, Atchison, KS, 1935.

*RB: 1980 The Rule of St. Benedict in English* ed. Timothy Fry, OSB, Liturgical Press, Collegeville, MN, 1981.

*A Reader's Version of the Rule of Saint Benedict in Inclusive Language,* a transliteration edited and adapted by Marilyn Schauble, OSB, and Barbara Wojciak, Benedictine Sisters of Erie, Erie, PA, 1989.

*Acknowledgments*

D on't be fooled: books are not a solitary enterprise. Oh, the writing is, of course, but the process itself is a complex one. Eliminate any part of the enterprise and the work itself is in doubt. For that, every writer must be consciously grateful. And I am.

I'm grateful in a special way for my editor, Gary Jansen, whose ear for what the world needs most to think about is both reassuring and energizing.

I'm forever grateful to my Benedictine community of sisters who make it possible for me to write and whose work on that behalf has been at least as much as my own.

I'm always grateful for my assistant, Susan Doubet, OSB, whose work on the preparation of the manuscript is thorough, precise, and faithful. Always.

Finally, I'm grateful for the bank of readers who think through the ideas with me in a very special and real way by simply reading the manuscript for me before it's published and are honest about what they find—or do not find there.

In the end, then, it is the effect of a book on a reader that measures the scope of its impact, the depth of its wisdom, the range of its meaning. Writing, in other words, is a kind of spiritual collaboration between the writer and the reader. What a writer describes, readers test against their own insights and sentience. It's that testing that determines the electricity between writers and their readership.

The readers who worked their way through *Radical Spirit* were particularly important. After all, this is a book written on three levels—the autobiographical, the social-psychological, and the spiritual—about feelings and issues and spiritual depth. These readers tested their questions, their experiences, and their own spiritual insights against the manuscript and helped me flesh it out on every level.

The readers who gave so much of themselves to this text are: Susan Doubet, OSB, Kathleen Felong, Harry Finkbone, Gail Freyne, Darcy Johnson, Mary Lou Kownacki, OSB, Annette Marshall, OSB, Anne McCarthy, OSB, Breanna Mekuly, Kathleen Schatzberg, Jacqueline Small, and Nancy Small.

For all of that I'm deeply grateful.

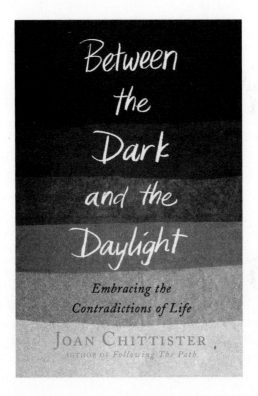

Between
the
Dark
and the
Daylight

*Embracing the
Contradictions of Life*

JOAN CHITTISTER
AUTHOR OF *Following The Path*